Change Your Life with Accelerated Visualisation

Change Your Life with Accelerated Visualisation

HAROLD KAMPF

With a Foreword by Colin Wilson

quantum

LONDON • NEW YORK • TORONTO • SYDNEY

quantum

An imprint of W. Foulsham & Co. Ltd
The Publishing House, Bennetts Close,
Cippenham, Slough, Berkshire, SL1 5AP, England

ISBN 0–572–02458–4

Previously published under the title
The Speed Technique to Alpha Meditation and Visualisation.

*The greatest discovery in our generation is that human beings,
by changing the inner attitudes of their minds, can change the
outer aspects of their lives.*

William James

Printed in Great Britain by St. Edmundsbury Press, Bury St. Edmunds, Suffolk.

Contents

Foreword

Harold Kampf is a personnel manager by trade, a writer by inclination – he has published ten books, mostly novels. In 1975, he sent me a small book of his on meditation. My initial reaction was rather negative – I am not fond of 'How to Do It' books on meditation, yoga, self-hypnosis and so on. But as soon as I casually opened the book, I knew this one was different. He was obviously a man who knew exactly what he was talking about. I happened to open it at a paragraph labelled 'Seeing Angels', and this intrigued me. Mr Kampf had apparently become interested in the techniques of Subud, that intriguing system of meditation developed in Indonesia by Pak Subuh. The essence of Subud is a method called the latihan, an 'opening up' of the mind that permits divine energies to operate. Harold Kampf was admitted to the latihan by a man who had been initiated by Subuh himself. Subuh seems to have been able to transmit some kind of current of vital energy, as had the Russian mystic Gurdjieff, who taught at his centre in Paris that his followers should look for the awakening of a higher consciousness beyond thought.

An English Moslem, Husein Rofe, first introduced Subud to John Bennett, a Gurdjieff follower in England, and it then spread through the UK to the US and other countries. John Bennett declared that he saw angels during the latihan. Kampf commented:

> 'No, really, I thought! This is a strain on credibility. And one evening during latihan I too saw angels. I hardly dare to set it down – yet I know it was so, even though my two angels were quite unlike angels I might have imagined. They were like Grecian temple maidens, clothed in shimmering blue. In the latihan I was not overawed, but calmly accepted their appearance as quite a natural and understandable thing.'

A man who could admit to seeing angels without embarrassment was obviously a down-to-earth sort of person, so I turned to the beginning of the book and found that Mr Kampf was indeed the kind of person I could trust – a man who had read a lot about meditation as well as practising it, and who knew what all the authorities had to say.

Another thing that interested me was that he attached basic importance to the idea of God without being, apparently, in any sense 'religious'. For Kampf, God was the creative energy of the universe, the Life Force. This again was refreshing. It still seems to me self-evidently true that the basic drive behind the force we call life is the desire to create deeper consciousness, a mirror in which it can become aware of itself. In Harold Kampf's world-view I immediately sensed something strongly akin to my own.

In fact, I came upon my own name in his book. After citing a semi-mystical experience of the nature writer Richard Jefferies, he mentions that these sensations were what the psychologist Abraham Maslow (about whom I wrote a book) called 'peak experiences'.

The passage of Jefferies he mentions is more than a mere description of a 'peak experience' – which Maslow defined as simply an experience of bubbling, overflowing happiness. Jefferies says:

> 'Sometimes I have concentrated myself, and driven away by continued will all sense of outward appearances, looking straight with the full power of my mind inwards on myself. I find "I" am there; an "I" I do not wholly understand or know … Recognising it, I feel on the margin of a life unknown … on the verge of powers

which if I could grasp could give me an immense breadth of existence, an ability to execute what I now only conceive.'

However, the Scottish philosopher David Hume stated that when he looked inside himself for the 'real David Hume' he merely glimpsed a lot of ideas and impressions. For the next two centuries, Hume's denial of the 'essential self' became a cornerstone of Western philosophy; everybody took it for granted – at least until the advent of a remarkable German thinker, Edmund Husserl, who pointed out that when we look at something, we fire our attention at it as an archer fires an arrow. If you let your attention drift as you read this page, you will simply fail to take it in – and that is as if the archer was too tired or lazy to pull back the bowstring and the arrow fell in front of him to the ground. And a bow and arrow implies an archer, an 'I' who fires the arrow. Apparently, Richard Jefferies had the ability to look deep inside himself and catch a glimpse of the archer who hides behind the façade of consciousness – the being Kant called the 'transcendental ego'.

This is an important insight. It means that if David Hume failed to see the archer when he looked inside himself, it was because he was not making the same effort that Jefferies made. In Robert Anton Wilson's book *Illuminatus*, someone remarks to a sage that when he looks inside himself he cannot see his essential 'self'; the sage replies:

'Who is doing the looking?'

Here we begin to move into the realm of Buddhistic insight, the sudden moment of enlightenment when we grasp the fact that we are not mere passive creatures of circumstance, leaves blown on the wind. We have real power to act, to do. And this is again a central recognition of an important philosopher: the German Fichte, a contemporary and follower of Kant. Fichte noticed that when we sit, merely thinking, we often feel like a total nonentity. (Everyone has had that experience of reading for much too long – or watching television – and beginning to experience a sense of utter collapse, a feeling of suffocation.) But the moment we launch ourselves into determined action, this sense of boredom and suffocation vanishes; we each feel a real person once more.

This is the feeling that all good teachers induce in their pupils – and it applies particularly to teachers of ideas. And it is something I felt as soon as I began to read the typescript of this new book by Harold Kampf.

Kampf soon makes us aware that in order to know certain basic secrets about living our lives we do not need to be some kind of an 'adept'. The secret itself is what matters, and it really works.

I found myself reading the book with increasing excitement. It brought back to me my own 'initiation' into such matters, at the age of 17. I was a typical adolescent intellectual, reading everything I could lay my hands on, yet always feeling bored, inadequate and clumsy. Like T.E. Lawrence, I envied a soldier with his girl, or a man patting his dog, because they seemed to belong to the real world, to nature, not to some intellectual twilight zone. Then, through a reference in one of T.S. Eliot's essays, I came across the *Bhagavadgita*, the Hindu scripture that teaches how a man should learn to know himself. The hero, Arjuna, is about to lead his army into battle against an army in which there are many of his friends and relatives; he bursts into tears and says he cannot do it. Then his teacher, Krishna, tells him that his mind is worried and confused by illusions. He must exercise total detachment and cease to care about the results of his actions. The only way to avoid suffering is to rise above the confusion of desires and anxieties that seem to constitute the warp and weft of human life. He must recognise that his essential being is immortal, made of the same substance as God.

I began to practise meditation, as taught in the *Gita*. I learnt to regard the adolescent 'me', trapped in his sense of awkwardness and incompetence, as a kind of illusion. Recognising that a part of my sense of will-lessness was due to inactivity, I began getting up early in the morning and jogging for an hour, then walking to work instead of taking the bus. The result was that I had a sudden sense of control over myself and my own life. I felt I was changing myself, turning myself into a different person. Whenever I had a chance, I would find a quiet place and sit cross-legged, my attention concentrated, my gaze 'fixed at the root of the eyebrows'. And it was like 'pulling myself together'; after ten minutes, I felt refreshed and full of energy.

There are, I later discovered, many different methods and systems of achieving some degree of self-control. I found that the Christian mysticism of Eckhart and Suso led in precisely the same direction as the serene meditation of Buddhism or Taoism – or, for that matter, the shock tactics of Zen. I realised that Socrates was aiming at the same kind of detachment through the use of the powers of reason, and that Marcus Aurelius achieved it through Stoic disciplines. And when I came upon Gurdjieff – in Ouspensky's *In Search of the Miraculous*, I realised that he attempted to combine many forms of discipline in his notion of self-observation and 'the war against sleep'. It made no difference which way one chose. The really important moment was the recognition that we can choose to alter ourselves, that even though all our habits of thought try to conceal it from us, we are masters of our own lives.

The way of Nietzsche's Zarathustra may seem very different from the way of St John of the Cross, but they are based upon the same optimistic insight: that we are stronger than we think. We do not have to be slaves of the trivial; the mind can be turned, like a searchlight, on to more important things.

H.G. Wells's Mr Polly said:

'If you don't like your life, you can change it.'

And the corollary is:

'If you don't like yourself, you can change that too.'

Then why bother to read *Change Your Life with Accelerated Visualisation* when the way to inner freedom has been known for thousands of years? Because our age has seen immense advances in the knowledge of the actual mechanisms of the mind. For example, we now know that the brain has two hemispheres, each one focusing on different aspects of our personality and activities.

It would be absurd to say:

'I don't want to know about such things because Socrates or Buddha did very well without them …'

What Harold Kampf has accomplished here is an exciting – and totally personal – synthesis of techniques that seem to range from traditional yoga to the visualising disciplines of the Cabbalah and the relaxation techniques of transcendental meditation. No one – no matter how much they know about such things – can fail to gain new insights from it.

The down-to-earth Mr Kampf has brought a refreshing new approach to one of mankind's oldest problems; that, in itself, is a life's achievement.

Colin Wilson

ONE

Why Do It?

Cabbage or Coleslaw?

Basically coleslaw is cabbage with mayonnaise added, plus a few simple refinements to make it even better and tastier. But it is still cabbage at heart.

Do you want to remain cabbage or become coleslaw?

Most people have wanted to change something about themselves at some stage of their lives. They don't want to change basically, just lose or change bad habits or improve their image – become more likeable, attractive, confident; improve their ability to perform – as a worker, an artist, a musician, a writer; play sport better, be healthier …

Anyone can achieve any of these things and the simplest, easiest way is by visualisation, being able to conjure up in your mind a picture of what you want to achieve that is so real that it gives you the impetus to achieve that state.

There are many books that will explain visualisation and tell you simply to visualise things, or to sit and breathe in this or that way in the hope that one day, with patience, you will achieve a meditative state. They may suggest you concentrate on your breathing, stare at a candle flame, imagine one colour and then another … and so on.

I have tried them all. None of them worked because visualisation is only truly effective if done in alpha, the state of relaxation in which our brain rhythms are slower and our awareness is enhanced. So eventually, almost despairingly, I devised my own whole person, deep level technique, the formula for which will appear later in this book, and taught it with some success. However, I then discovered another method, which I call the ABC method, and as soon as I had done so, I realised that this was the ultimate way to achieve the alpha state speedily and easily. This technique is also described in this book. Whichever route I took to achieve the alpha state, I could meditate and visualise to change my life.

Anyone can decide they want to change something about themselves and make assertions such as:

> *'I am calmer, nothing can affect my equilibrium.'*
>
> *'I am becoming less irritable every day.'*
>
> *'My heartbeat is calm and regular.'*
>
> *'My warts are disappearing.'*
>
> *'My golf swing is improving every day.'*

But just imagine how many hundred times more effective those statements must be if at the same time you 'see' in your mind these improvements taking place. When you do this at the alpha level, what you 'see' is what you can become.

What Is Alpha?

The rhythm of activity in the brain varies depending on your mental state. You probably know the recognised brain rhythms of beta, alpha, theta and delta.

Beta is our normal waking state, when the speed of the brain rhythm is 13 to 40 cycles per second.

Alpha is a slower rhythm, at 8 to 13 cycles per second. This state is normally attained in meditation and hypnosis. Although slower, being in the alpha state involves a heightened sense of awareness so it is the ideal state in which to practise meditation and visualisation.

Theta often overlaps with alpha and is the next deeper state, the speed being 4 to 7 cycles per second. Theta can then overlap with delta, which is the usual sleep state. The speed of delta rhythm is 0.5 to 3 cycles per second.

De-mystification of Meditation

The main purpose of this book is to de-mystify the subjects of meditation and visualisation and to set out how to achieve a state of meditation in the fastest possible way.

Why fast? Because many people are put off trying meditation and visualisation because they think they are confusing and complicated, and because some practitioners advocate methods that don't work or methods that require long exercises to reach a meditative state. Some teachers feel it is important to take time to learn the techniques in order to prove one's seriousness, if nothing else. They contend that it is only when you are prepared to spend time that you deserve the prize of self-help.

I believe otherwise. I believe that the more people there are who practise meditation, the better the world will become. In this book, I will cover both passive meditation, for relaxation and stress relief, and dynamic meditation, the method by which you can make changes in yourself and your life. Both have great advantages and can help make your life better.

Our Masks and Our Real Selves

The Sufis claim that everything we experience in life is a stepping stone to achieving life's inner purpose. The chief aspects of that purpose are the desire to live, to gain knowledge, to attain power, happiness and peace. I would interpret that as power over one's self rather than power over others.

Despite the fact that the world is full of multitudes of people, in some ways it is rather a lonely world. At times we wonder why we are here and whether life is a joke, an accident or perhaps merely a creative experiment. We ask ourselves whether existence has any real purpose or meaning. To many people, life appears to be one long struggle with little reward once the security of our childhood fades away – and even that security does not exist for some. Certainly, we live and work together for mutual benefit and comfort, but because of the way we've structured the world we are all increasingly in competition. Everyone wants to be the biggest or the best, the most beautiful, the most influential or powerful. If we do not succeed, we pretend not to care. Whatever our situation, we adopt personae to help us get through our lives. We hide our real selves behind masks to give us confidence, because we feel too vulnerable without them.

Harvey Stack Sullivan, the respected psychologist, called such masks our 'security operations', designed to reduce our vulnerability and protect already damaged egos. For example, a sensitive person who is afraid of being hurt may wear a sardonic, callous mask, giving the impression that they are tough. That may offer a degree of protection but it does not change their sensitive nature; behind the mask they can still be hurt. And because these masks prevent others getting to know us properly – getting to know the real person with all the fears and uncertainties we all have – behind our masks we are likely to feel a certain emptiness and a need for reassurance.

We decide that in order to gain what we need to be happy, we have to act in certain ways. We behave in such a way as to show others the kind of person we want them to think we are – we wear the relevant mask in different sets of circumstances. Unfortunately, because we are not always projecting our real selves, we sometimes give the wrong impression; we don't paint on our masks very successfully. And, of course, other people don't always read our masks properly and so come to the wrong conclusions about us.

Negative Emotions

Perhaps our most basic emotion is fear, since everything else seems to spring from it. Fear is basic self-protection; we tend to run from anything which might harm us, physically and emotionally. Even emotions such as love can only come after fear has been conquered – fear of rejection, fear of being hurt – and trust has been established.

Another strong human emotion is desire – wanting what we don't have – that's fairly basic too. Desire also starts right down from our most fundamental needs of food and shelter and moves up the scale to wanting the regard and esteem of others. Desire can be positive; we cannot achieve a goal without really wanting it to happen and believing it will happen. However, it can become negative if instead of using it to spur us on to achieve worthy goals, we let it degrade into covetousness.

Other emotions, such as resentment and anger, can spring from many causes, most usually when other people don't react to us, or our masks, in the way we want them to. Resentment and anger are both terribly destructive emotions. You may have heard someone saying with pride, 'I get angry very quickly' – when I do, I shudder for the speaker.

What wonderful lives we could all have if we were free from those three monsters: fear, desire and anger.

Pride is an offshoot of desire and fear. If we weren't afraid of being thought inferior, unworthy, we wouldn't trouble to wear a mask of pride.

A wise man once said:

> 'He is truly liberated who is free from desire, fear and anger.'

Very few people could claim to have achieved that state but it must be something to which we all aspire.

Main Aims in Life

Someone has said that our main aims in life are to avoid pain and to experience pleasure. Pain, whether mental or physical, is to be feared and avoided while pleasure is to be actively sought.

But what is pleasure? Is it love, security, comfort, status? Many people think of it as a single objective: for example a visit to the theatre or cinema, the act of getting married, falling in love or into bed, a football match, a party. Yet in fact every single objective of pleasure, once it has been reached, no longer satisfies. There is only one permanent satisfier: a feeling of serene joy or real contentment experienced at the very core of our lives. But is that a true possibility?

It is for many people, if they want it enough. We are not, of course, all at the same stage of development but a tremendous number of people are ready to live in peace and happiness, if only they could learn to improve the quality of their lives. There are those who argue that if we had no conflict or competition, life would be boring and there would be no progress. I believe that this is a specious argument for we are born with great curiosity and an imaginative and creative urge, and being happy frees and enhances our ability to exercise those qualities. One might enquire whether our Creator requires conflict to be creative.

What then, are we to make, of evil? Is there not always the conflict of good versus evil? How does this concept fall into place in our quest for understanding?

Those who have heard or read the mystic teacher and writer Paul Solomon may remember that when his spiritual 'guides' were asked to define God they said it was 'the power that could envisage good without reference to evil'. Do you follow the concept? It does not involve the usual balance of good versus evil; good exists as a quite separate entity.

When I use passive meditation I say to myself, 'There is only God; there is only God's power,' by which I mean that I do not believe that any evil force can exist unless we accept it as a separate force and, by doing so, grant it power. I believe this mantra protects me from the concept of evil.

So how do we understand the concept of good? Christ commanded us to love one another and gave us the golden rule:

'Do unto others as you would have them do unto you.'

From this I devised my own karmic rule:

'Whatever you do unto others will be done unto you.'

Confucius had a similar rule of reciprocity, called *shu* in Chinese: 'Do not do unto others what you do not want others to do unto you.' They all amount to very much the same thing and make sense even if we view them in very basic terms, but they are even easier to understand if we happen to believe we are all part of one great consciousness.

What is Love?

Going back to our most basic emotions, we found that fear was the start of everything. In our fear-ridden society, how then do we go about casting out fear? How do we stop being afraid? In the Christian scriptures, it says, 'Perfect love casteth out fear'.

If we accept that love removes fear, we have to ask what love is. My dictionary defines it as an intense emotion of affection, warmth, fondness and regard towards a person or thing. Sometimes this is easy: we have no difficulty loving our children or loving things that make our lives better. But perfect love? Can we really feel this emotion about everyone and everything around us? To aim at this one would have to emulate Mother Teresa, a difficult task indeed. She might even have tended an ailing Hitler with concern, whereas most of us would consign him for ever to outer darkness.

So let's not try to move too far too quickly; we are human, after all, and have our limitations. But we can at least start moving in the right direction by consciously looking for the good qualities in the people we meet and trying not to focus on qualities, such as ignorance or pride, that make them seem unlovable. Even the worst people have redeeming traits in their character; try to find them. Often, exercising sympathy and understanding can open the door to loving. If you can love the parts of someone which are lovable, this gives space for what is not lovable in them to change. We have to make the first move and it is not so difficult, after all, to start sending out affection, warmth and regard to others.

If one could achieve a state of mind in which one were always loving – always sending out positive feelings and looking for the good in others – one would be at peace. It would be impossible to be greedy, or to want what someone else had. One would be so secure in oneself that there could be nothing to fear.

The Process of Change

To start this process of developing a more loving nature, one needs to change. Simple? Or not?

Happiness, remember, is freedom from fear, desire and anger. And we experience all three of these emotions as a result of interacting with others: from what other people do or say, from their reactions to us or our reactions to them. But although our problem may at first seem to be other people, it is in fact our own reaction to other people. It is wanting something from others – be it approval, security, sex or whatever. That's what gives others the power to hurt us, by not behaving in the way that we want. Just think about wanting something badly and not getting it – whether it's approval, or promotion or even love – that's what hurts us. Yet whatever it is we want, we don't really need it. It is not essential for survival or happiness because the only true happiness, the only true security comes from within. We cannot change or control the behaviour of others. We can only be truly responsible for our own behaviour. It follows, then, that if we want true happiness, we must find it in ourselves.

If we continue to be competitive and demanding, we will not be happy because there will always be something else we desire. What we need to realise is that if and when we finally get what we've been demanding, we still won't be happy. For a short while we may feel very pleased. Then we soon find something else to aim for and become dissatisfied again until we achieve it. We can stay trapped in this cycle unless we begin to realise that short-term pleasure is not true happiness. If we chase happiness, when we've caught it – why, it's gone again: 'to catch the winged joy as it flies …' as William Blake put it. True happiness can only come from within and to be truly happy is to be yourself always, not to have hunger for approval, for acceptance. To be happy is to be content in every moment – that is real freedom.

Happiness

Happiness is inner freedom from fear, anger and anxiety. It has nothing to do with anyone else; no one can either give it to you or withdraw it from you. When you give up your dependency on others you become independent and confident. When you are at peace within yourself, you are freed from what others think or do; you alone are in charge. You have enough and you do not covet the riches or glamour of others.

But some believe that we are bound to strive for more. Did not Christ, they ask, rebuke the man who made little use of his talents?

Strive for more of what? Not money, not goods, not sex, not material things! Only immaterial things such as knowledge, wisdom, love and an improvement of your talents. For every one of us has some special talents, something unique to offer. What we have to do is to recognise them, then foster and develop them so that we do the absolute best we can with them. It doesn't have to be a big talent – we're not all going to be concert pianists. It doesn't necessarily even mean that sort of talent. You might have a talent for communicating well with children, for being a good mother, for being a good messenger – or even a lavatory cleaner for that matter.

We should never envy those who seem rich or strong; they only seem so, but in some other way they too may be weak and suffering. Perhaps they have poor health, or are unhappy at home. They all wear masks too, to hide their real selves and in particular to hide their vulnerability. But when a person appears who has inner strength and conviction, it is easy to see that such a person has no need to wear a mask. Because they neither want nor need what other people have, they can afford to be their real selves and by doing so, they make those who wear masks seem insecure by contrast.

So if that inner happiness is the goal for which we want to strive, we need to start a process of change. There comes a time when we just have to sit down quietly and be analytical and, most of all, honest about ourselves. We shall talk more later on about self-analysis and essential goals. However, if we're seriously considering some sort of change in ourselves, then we must first face ourselves honestly and truthfully. Who are we? What are our strengths and weaknesses? What are we really like?

Then we must take a good, calm look and examine our inner goals. We must not strive to be a powerful business manager but to be at peace. We will not achieve happiness if we aim to be successful, since success is a totally objective-based concept – once we have achieved what we are striving for, the next objective will present itself further on. We can achieve happiness only if we aim to be in harmony with the universe. We need not only to do what we want but also to want what we do, to do our best work and to be a loving person.

Our Inner Goals

At this point, we should summarise our goals:

- To rid ourselves of our old ideologies.

- To heal ourselves emotionally and spiritually.

- To be our true selves, healthy in mind and ways, independent but having good relationships with others.

If we can achieve these things, it will bring us permanent peace, happiness and an abiding contentment. Could one ask for more?

Possibly not – but we may question whether contentment supplies a reason for living. The answer is 'not really', though we are likely to come to a reason when our mind is at peace, because then we become aware of a force beyond ourselves. It is possible to live peacefully even when we believe life to be an accident. But when we realise that life leans towards good rather than evil, when we examine ourselves and see our need to develop harmoniously, then we probably are here to do just that, to grow.

Inner Growth

Growth is learning. A first step might be to recognise when we do wrong – to be aware when we are doing something 'ugly', as a child I know put it so beautifully. But to know we are doing something ugly and just not care, that's hardly a forward step. So we grow mainly in our attitudes towards others, in consideration, in compassion, in unselfishness.

It is difficult to be unselfish and caring when you are unhappy. But, of course, we are unhappy when we are at odds: desiring, fearful, anxious, resentful, angry. So, again, if we are not afraid of whatever anyone says or does, then we no longer desire, become fearful, anxious, resentful or angry.

Can we really remake ourselves, in effect create our own lives afresh? Yes, we can – almost like an artist creating a picture from scratch. People often blame their parents, their inherited genes and their environment for their faults and, of course, these conditions may have been formative factors. However, there comes a time when we have to say: 'I'm on my own. What's past is past but I'm starting afresh right now, and from now on it's up to me.' After that, we have a wonderful blank piece of paper on which to redraw. That is easy enough to say, but it does mean giving up the bad habits of a lifetime.

A Case History

Before I start to explain the mechanics of change – how you can actually go about it – it might be useful to look at a case history. This is the story of Kathy.

Kathy was troubled about her marriage to Harry because she felt that he had lost interest in her. The way she put it was that she felt she was losing her identity.

Now when things go wrong in a relationship, when there is disagreement, many women want to talk it through, analyse and digest it and give the situation a good workout. Men, on the other hand, often don't feel comfortable with this. If there has been a specific disagreement – an argument or whatever – then, once it is over, they would rather put it behind them and carry on as before. They don't want to go back and talk about it. Unfortunately their partner can, and often does, see that as a lack of interest. Over small matters, most couples can get used to such differences of approach and learn compromise and, perhaps, a little understanding of the other's position. However, if misunderstanding is allowed to continue, it can become very serious.

Kathy was sensitive not only to her husband's behaviour but also to that of her friends and relatives. She was very close to her father, despite the fact that he was a big drinker and she did not like either his appetite for alcohol or his behaviour when he became drunk. This became the catalyst which brought the situation to a head.

Kathy's father had embarrassed Harry when Harry had taken him to a special function. Harry had been furious at the time not only with her father but, by association, with Kathy herself. Kathy spent a sleepless night, angry with her father and feeling guilty towards Harry because her father had caused all the trouble just when Harry was trying to be especially nice to him.

By the morning, however, Harry had got over his anger. Kathy, on the other hand, couldn't wait to talk it all out with her husband. But what did he do when she raised the issue? He looked surprised and touched her gently on the shoulder in sympathy, but as far as he was concerned the matter was finished; he didn't want to discuss it. He was even more surprised when she then burst into tears. From her point of view it was obvious that if he didn't want to discuss something of such importance in their marriage – something which had caused him such rage at the time – then their relationship couldn't mean much to him. The pattern was always the same; he was simply never interested in her point of view.

Kathy was being swept along by the words, actions and reactions of Harry and everybody else. When other people couldn't understand how she felt about things, she felt hurt, misunderstood and unsure of herself. She was very often in this unhappy state. Since she and Harry also ran a business together, she could not get away from the conflict and even professionally they were becoming adversaries.

So Kathy set about changing things. First she analysed herself and decided what were her assets and liabilities. Her main asset, she felt, was her looks since she was a very attractive woman. But this was just a freak of nature and didn't help her anyway, she reasoned. In fact, sometimes it was a disadvantage as people often thought that confidence went with good looks, whereas she often felt lonely and uncertain. Next, she was kind and generally felt goodwill towards people, until she was rebuffed. She had quite a good brain and a nice husband – except that she wasn't sure he really cared about her.

What were her liabilities? She felt they were twofold: a lack of confidence, and too great a dependence, first on her father and then on her husband. This led to anger and resentment when they did anything to upset her, and a constant uneasy fear that something would transpire to break the calm. Because of her fear, she was nervy and short-tempered with Harry and continually on the defensive. This attitude put him on the defensive and made him keep a distance between them, resorting to sarcasm as a weapon.

Kathy realised that she could not change other people, only herself, and the first stage in changing and improving things was to calm herself, both physically and mentally. She learnt how to do this – we shall discover the method later on. She also realised she had to learn emotional independence. She had to be her true self and be happy with herself as she really was. She would be as nice looking as she could, at peace with herself, unselfish, able to use her mind constructively and creatively (as indeed she could when it was uncluttered with negative emotions), thoughtful, considerate and caring. Those were her real values and in time they also became her face value.

Finding Ourselves

Kathy's problem was the one we all face. It was the question of: 'Who am I?' All her life she had allowed herself to be dependent on other people. She had wanted their understanding, their approval, because she did not really approve of herself. This actually put her in their power. They had not asked for this power but she gave it to them because subconsciously she thought that was what she needed. When she analysed the situation, she discovered that this was not what she needed at all; in fact, relying on other people for one's own self-esteem can never lead to happiness, so she consciously withdrew that power from them. In effect she said: 'From now on I'm going to conform to my own standards and you must accept me as I am. If you reject me, that's okay with me.'

She became strong enough to be able to say that. She realised that when you detach yourself from others in this way they lose their power over you, that when you are complete, happy, joyful and loving, no one can disturb you, and that if they do it is only because you give them the power to affect you.

It is rather like driving a car. Whatever apparently senseless thing (short of hitting you) that another driver does, it can only affect you if you give your permission. If you react, who does it affect? You. Your anger will hurt you but certainly not the other driver. If you think calmly: 'Poor soul! I feel sorry that he has to act like that; I'll try to send him some good vibrations and maybe he'll feel better,' then you are in charge of the situation. Anger is one's own worst enemy, affecting the angry person much more adversely than the recipient.

It wasn't easy at first for Kathy to establish a distance between herself and others. But she learnt to 'watch' a painful emotion reaching her – anger, distress, fear, hurt – and then continue to watch it and deliberately withdraw from it so it would lose its power over her. The more she could control her emotions, the more power she had. She learnt to listen to people properly and to try to understand what was really happening between them and herself. When she neither expected nor demanded any special form of behaviour from them, she could never be disappointed. When she did not impose her standards on others, she became more self-contained, more understanding and less judgmental. She learnt not to respond to people in a personal or emotional way. She was at last able to be herself, unique (as we all are) and genuine.

Since this is an important aim for all of us, let's look now at the first stage of the process and see how we can actually begin to achieve this sense of peace.

TWO

How It Works

Relaxation

We have established that the best way to relax completely is to reach a state in which the brain rhythms are functioning in alpha. To achieve alpha requires relaxation of both the body and the brain. You will notice that I say brain and not mind. Mind is in total charge; it is you. It is mind that gives direction to the brain and the brain then instructs the body. Your mind is your 'director'; if you believe in immortality, we might describe your mind as your immortal essence.

You may wonder why it is necessary to relax physically and the answer is that unless you do, you cannot get the brain to relax. Another reason (part of the same, really) is the need to do away with tension or stress. When your body and brain are tense, you cannot be calm and slip into alpha. This is why it is so difficult to go into alpha when you are troubled or in pain. However, if you have learnt the technique and become accustomed to meditating regularly, you will be able to use that technique to relax and go into alpha in times of stress and so alleviate the situation.

Stress

Since stress is one of the things we are aiming to control, we need to define what it is and how to avoid too much of it. Stress is a natural part of everyday life and a little stress is not necessarily a bad thing. It is part of our basic survival mechanism. If we were all completely 'laid back', nothing would ever get done!

High levels of stress or tension, however, seem to be a part of modern living and can affect you adversely by causing chemical changes in the body, in particular in the brain. Too much stress can weaken the body's immune system, for example, leaving you susceptible to colds or other viral infections. It can aggravate illnesses such as irritable bowel syndrome, give you muscular aches such as backache, or even give you headaches.

Stress affects not only people with high-pressure jobs, although obviously the constant and sometimes unreasonable demands placed on business executives make them prime targets for stress-related problems. It can and does affect everyone, even those in jobs which are apparently undemanding. It may even be the very fact that their jobs do not involve any decision-making that means some people find them stressful.

Stress can also be caused by hostility, by a single, major problem or simply by many small daily irritations. You may become stressed even without your conscious knowledge, by polluted air, by too much constant noise, by all the hazards of overcrowding, by fierce and relentless competition. Feelings of anxiety, low self-esteem, phobias, inability to cope, poor concentration and memory, depression – all these can result from too much stress or tension.

Daily relaxation of your brain and body by meditation can counteract the causes of stress in your environment and help you to remain calm. When you are calm, you can begin to take charge of your life, instead of being controlled by circumstances, and that is the first step towards improving both your quality of life and your health. It pays to develop a technique for relaxation, and I will explain the method I use on page 62. It pays even more benefit if you then meditate, and again I'll give you full instructions later.

Types of Meditation

Originally, to meditate meant to exercise the mind in contemplation, to think about a subject and turn it inside out, to contemplate it deeply. Gradually, it acquired a religious connotation and a meaning which is quite the reverse of actually thinking about anything at all. I believe it means giving one's mind over to God. I use the word 'God', but you can substitute whatever word for a higher power fits with your own religious beliefs or philosophy. Because of that definition, I do not believe that you can achieve true meditation if you do not believe in a higher power, and I will discuss this further in the next chapter. You can certainly still go into alpha, relax your body and brain and get in touch with a deeper, subconscious self. All these things will have benefits, but I believe will only take you so far.

In passive meditation, you go into alpha and relax both your brain and your body. In handing over your mind to the power of God, you make contact with your deeper, subconscious self.

With dynamic meditation, you are consciously using your mind at that deeper level to instruct your body and brain to work on yourself, to improve yourself and make yourself better in some way. In time you can expand your awareness, improve your creativity and find yourself more at peace. Because you will become calmer, you are likely to be healthier and more relaxed.

Doctors confirm that effective meditation can help to repair an immune system damaged by stress, as well as having other positive physical effects. Physical relaxation is comparatively easy but the 'psychological dimension' eludes many people, and meditation helps to provide this missing dimension since it provides very deep levels of rest in both a physical and psychological sense.

Some people who have been addicted to drugs have found that they can kick the habit with the help of meditation. Those who had not believed in an external higher power but felt a subconscious need for that belief, have discovered that they can take the 'leap of faith'. On the other hand, those who do not feel the need for a spiritual dimension in their lives need not fear being inveigled into spirituality. God is a closed shop and membership is open only to those who seek it.

'What is there capable of surviving the cataclysm of death?' asks Kenneth Walker in My Key to Life. 'Only in moments of meditation when the everyday self is momentarily in abeyance do I catch a glimpse of the greater self, which is entirely different from the small, separate self of everyday life.'

The Need for Meditation

Do we need meditation? Is this contact with a higher power – or even a higher self – something which we should seek out?

I always consider myself extremely fortunate in having had a 'conversion experience' many years ago when I was in great personal need. While I was in a state of despair, an inner voice suddenly expressed itself by telling me not to worry, to 'let go' and all would be well in due time. This experience was blindingly clear and real to me and I instantly knew that, contrary to my previous belief, life was part of an immortality, that physical death was merely the first step on the way and that I was undoubtedly in the hands of higher forces than my own.

Without this knowledge, I cannot think that I would so happily have succumbed to the modern world in which we live. But since then, supporting evidence from the body of occult literature has accumulated so quickly that it is there for anyone to acquire. And if you meditate regularly with an open mind, jagged shafts of light constantly hurl themselves at you and enlarge your understanding.

Meditation and Prayer

What's more, to meditate, you don't actually have to do anything. As Brother Mandus, a writer in mysticism, said in *This Wondrous Way of Life:*

'There is nothing to do! The Father does all that needs to be done. I say silently: "Here is my life, Father, all I am, all I possess; I lay it down for Thee. This moment, this day, eternally, Thy will, not mine." The silence in the Father's presence grows deeper as I practise coming to Him ... We should not ask God for anything in the silence; it is the time for God to do all that needs to be done. Our

only task is to allow Him to do it. If we do this it is absolutely amazing how all things for our joy are added upon us, pressed down and running over – love, wisdom, happiness, achievement, and supply.'

Could one ask for more?

As St Augustine said:

'I went round the streets and squares and cities of the world seeking Thee and found Thee not, because I sought without for Him who was within.'

Possibly the Christian Churches have forgotten the importance of meditation. A clergyman who read a previous book of mine *(In Search of Serenity)* on this subject said:

'It is such a pity we in the Church don't read and do more about this; we need to find the time.'

There is time enough for prayer but, in fact, true meditation is a deep form of prayer.

What is it to pray? It is to become one with God or with the Eternal. To pray is to talk, and the higher you go, the more silent your speech.

A well-known American seer spoke to me about an occasion when he was visiting a youngster in prison and speaking to him about religion. Later, when he visited the boy again, he found him kneeling and repeating the alphabet slowly from beginning to end. Curious, he asked the boy why he did this.

'Sir,' was the reply, *'if that man Jesus is as wise as you say, he knows better than me what I want to tell him.'*

We can see and sense the truth of this. If and when we pray it is usually to tell God what we want him to do for us. Isn't the best prayer perhaps: 'I leave it to you'?

The truest prayer, then, is the silent meditative communion with the creative force. You have taken yourself out of the way; you have made yourself ready to receive the power. You have come in silence and submission and you rest in stillness for whatever may appear.

When we are in meditation, we indeed speak within our inmost silence and release our field of energy, our consciousness, to the great life force. Following the law of all nature, what we give out returns to us in full measure and overflowing. As we know, this applies to both good and ill. Therefore if we open ourselves and release the flow of energy, we engender a return force which may at times make us feel that we are a veritable power house.

When you feel this for yourself you will come to understand how the meditation of a few can change the attitudes of the many. In deep, silent prayer or meditation, one finds that one goes beyond the need for purely personal gain and development. One finds contact with and joins the universal force of which all life is a part; one becomes a unity with it and with mankind as a whole. One becomes a channel, a sort of conduit through which the force can travel to all those who in any way come within one's consciousness.

An Easy Route to Meditation

Until now, meditation has always been considered complex and difficult to learn and has therefore often been avoided. Now the technique can be learnt quickly and easily. It is available to everyone who wants to try it. And in every religion it seems that meditation is found to be the one common factor necessary for spiritual progress. One might even say that without it one comes to a spiritual barrier: 'Thus far and no further!' We are like the man in the story of Christ's footprints:

One night a man had a dream. He dreamt he was walking along a beach with the Lord. Across the sky flashed scenes from his life. For each scene he noticed two sets of footprints in the sand: one belonging to him and the other to the Lord.

When the last scene of his life flashed before him he looked back at the footprints. He noticed that many times along the path of his life there was only one set of footprints. He also noticed that this happened at the very lowest and saddest times of his life. This really bothered him and he questioned the Lord about it.

'Lord, you said that once I decided to follow you, then you would walk with me all the way. But I have noticed that during the more troublesome times of my life there is only one set of footprints. I do

not understand why when I needed you most you would leave me all alone.'

The Lord replied: 'My son, my precious child, I love you and would never leave you. During your times of trial and suffering, when you see only one set of footprints, it was then that I carried you.'

THREE

The Trouble with God

God and Meditation

As I have said, it is my belief that true meditation puts us in touch with a higher power. For that reason, I feel it is essential to meet the question of spirituality head-on and discuss my understanding of God and the benefits I – and others who also believe – gain from meditation.

If you do not believe in a higher spritual dimension, then you may not be interested in this chapter. That's not a problem. Simply move on to the next. There is no reason why you should not learn to go quickly into alpha and attain a meditative state. Those who are interested in the concept of God, however, will find this chapter of benefit. And even if you don't share my views, it may be of interest to understand the further dimensions I believe everyone can achieve – if they truly want to.

If the name 'God' is a problem in itself, then there are many possible alternatives you can consider: universal intelligence, omnipotent mind, universal spirit or power, infinite intelligence. There are an endless number of alternatives; choose something which feels appropriate to you and your beliefs.

The real trouble with God is that so many people still see Him as an entity – a superhuman – but when we start to visualise God as a force, the life force that created and holds the universe together, then that's a different story. Another way of looking at it might be to say that God is law – the law of love, the law of creation, birth and rebirth – not an entity that can be contacted and asked for things (to refashion or renew relationships, to change circumstances, for example). The power for good – God – is always there, always available when we open ourselves to it.

Perhaps the most remarkable thing is that we can alienate ourselves from the power of good as much as we like, do as we wish, and yet when we finally open ourselves to it and call out to the power in our distress, it is always there waiting for us, offering itself to our acceptance; that is the real grace of God. Lawrence LeShan puts it well when he says:

> 'It seems to me that the challenge to science, to man, to the human experiment, is finally and irrevocably whether or not man can accept that he is a part of the energy of the universe and can only function harmoniously within it through his capacity to love infinitely.'

From *The Aquarian Conspiracy* comes this note:

> 'The more we learn about the nature of reality, the more plainly we see the unnatural aspects of our environment – and our lives. Out of ignorance, out of arrogance, we have been working against the grain ... Not realising that our species evolved in co-operation, we have opted for competition in work, school, relationships.'

And this is indeed our world – competitiveness, winning at all costs, achieving power and gaining possessions. The opposite is co-operation, harmony, service to those around us and the attempt to move towards unconditional love. It is a hard road to travel alone, perhaps impossible without the recognition of a power that's stronger than you. When you do move along this road, you strangely begin to get an almost automatic co-operation from others too. The reason is

THE TROUBLE WITH GOD

that you have then begun to be another sort of person, a loving and giving person.

A Meditative Experience

One day in meditation, I had the strange feeling of wanting to 'dissolve' myself. Somehow the sides of my body had seemed to start dissolving and, enjoying the feeling, I mentally encouraged my whole body to do the same until finally I was just 'not there'. I felt that I had become in a very real way a part of the universal life force. For a while after that, every time I meditated I began deliberately to repeat this experience. You could put it another way and say I placed my body on one side and surrendered my consciousness to becoming one with my source, or the one and only consciousness that we all are, that all things are. During these periods I deliberately linked up my consciousness with the source, and when you do this the power you feel is phenomenal – because you are not only part of it, you are it. To me it seemed that I had returned, for that period of time, to the power that created me and that this was really the answer to life.

Eileen Caddy is the co-founder of the Findhorn community in Scotland and the author of many books communicated to her by a higher power. She talks about a 'still, small voice' which is probably akin to 'the god within' which can be heard in meditation.

> 'Listen – listen – and then you cannot fail to hear that still, small voice within you which is my voice, and the most wondrous gift which I hold out to all mankind …'

For thousands of years we have been drifting away from the power, thus creating what I consider to be the only real sin there is: the sin of separation. This true sin does not compare, for me, with any worldly sins. We were made by the power as part of itself, and this is what is meant by mankind being created in God's image. Our job, our purpose, is to experience life in the world for the power, as an extension of itself. Everything is provided: health, an abundance of the necessities of life, physical resources – they are there for everyone who asks for them in the right way.

There really is enough for everyone, not when you ask, or petition, but when you *demand* it by law, which means living your life in accordance with the law of the universe and not merely by fulfilling your own desires.

However, when you choose to remain and live in separation from the source, you find a quality of life is lacking. Life has no real meaning. Sooner or later most people want to return to their source, although for some this can come too late. Although I believe that even if it is too late for this life, we all have another chance, another time, even another life.

Yet if you do hand over to God and say:

> *'I want you to live my life through me; please help me to get myself out of the way and just use me as a channel'*,

why, then it happens. Everything falls into place and your life becomes meaningful, and then you can just live from day to day because you have become a definite part of a plan – only it's not your plan. You have handed over, and your faith and trust are never misplaced. Do not take it on my word, but what can it cost you to experiment?

If you do try it, then whatever happens to you – and it may not be what you expected or even hoped for – will be right for you, the best thing possible for your growth and development (which is really what you are here for), and yes, even for your eventual enjoyment and satisfaction, for you will know you are a very real part of the divine plan.

There really has to be a divine plan, don't you think? Could all this intricacy of life be just an accident? Whatever nonsense there is in life can only ever be attributable to us, mankind, exercising our free will! That must be the ultimate argument for those who blame the Almighty for the Holocaust or other dreadful events in human history. Certainly, there are natural accidents in the world ('Acts of God', the insurers call them) and at times nature itself seems a little barbaric, but we can only try to understand ourselves and not the infinite. And finally, when you come to believe that life is eternal, our perspective on our present existence becomes quite different.

Happiness: the Inner Secret

You may remember the biblical instruction: 'Take no thought for the morrow.' When you do that it does not mean you now have to pack up your own goals. You still have these, only you may well find your goals have changed, or are changing, because of the new you now emerging. But you will be directed, put on the right path and required to carry on. You might think that now you have asked this power to run your life you need do nothing further yourself, but of course this is not so. Just because you have handed over the plan for your life, it does not mean the plan can be executed by anyone except you. What you have really been saying is:

'Show me what you want me to do, guide me and give me the means, the tools, to do it.'

Once you have effected this handover, you are in a position to feel completely at ease with yourself. Your internal state has nothing to do with other people; it concerns only the you within, the inner you. Being your own self now takes on a new meaning because it works in accordance with divine power and not merely your own. Being yourself in this way creates a self that is completely other: supportive, dependent not on peer wishes but on your new 'centred' self. Because you are now listening to your inner music, you no longer need to fear the tunes of other people. You can allow them to behave as they wish and you are free to be inner-confident, to be independent while also being caring and compassionate. You will no longer fear failure, sickness, loneliness. Paradoxically, because you have handed over, you actually have more power to deal with things, not less.

One might ask, if the law of the universe is impersonal and cannot be petitioned, how can it be ever called upon? The answer is that since it provides everything you can ever need, once you have accepted this and handed over yourself to the power – and not a minute before – you will draw to yourself everything you need in life. And you can actually claim it in this way:

'All power, all consciousness, is at the centre of my being always, and draws to me everything necessary for my good.'

If you say this daily in your meditation, it helps clear a channel for its fulfilment. And you yourself may be used (and be glad to be used) to send power and help to others.

How Does the Power Work?

So how does this power, this infinite mind or intelligence, work? We don't really know, of course, but we must believe there is some hierarchy of helpers – not too difficult to believe once we accept an afterlife of some sort.

Life is energy and the transfer of energy (whatever its nature), and when your mind is centred on the one power, the only power, that knows your good, then that power creates and materialises your positive desires – having indeed first created those very desires in your mind.

Thus handing over is the ultimate decision in your life. And what is it you really face? It can be a bit of a risk, can't it? After all, the whole thing may possibly be a fraud! It is because of this that people who live on logic alone just cannot do it, cannot accept it, cannot even think or talk about it. Their right-brain hemispheres of intuition and inner listening have atrophied. Yet even they have inner dreams, although they close their minds both to these and to the divinity that is within them. They live in sadness, in denial of their true selves.

Yes, it is a risk, a leap in the dark. But what tremendous rewards are on offer: love, acceptance, support, inner knowledge, no feverish struggle to achieve, only the calm of doing, daily achievement, growth. The achievement by itself is no longer vital; the doing is all, bringing satisfaction and contentment. Certainly, you must work towards your goals; nevertheless, you must not worry about the results, must set no demands, but just work harmoniously with hope, with optimism, with expectancy. When you do this you become freed, a free person. When all is well now, then it will be always well. The present moment is always now, not the past, not the future.

And if the results do not always appear good? That must not be allowed to matter. If one has done one's careful best, that is all that really matters and the appearance is not always the answer. Living in this way, worry falls behind and fear goes out of the window: all is proceeding as it should. You are under the control of infinite power, and away from the control of human power. You can actually declare: 'I give this situation no power over me.' Handing over does not diminish you in any way. You are not in competition with your source; you are its agent, its servant.

The trouble is that some people do not want to be a servant, even of God. 'Toughies!' as a friend of mine says. Delusions of grandeur have a limit, and this is it. After all, they came here for a purpose – to develop spiritually, to grow in awareness, to recognise and use 'the kingdom within'. People who are cruel and uncaring, who are all for self, can only destroy themselves and waste their lives. We can pity them because they do not know what they are doing to themselves. They are still asleep, unaware. They may have acquired worldly importance, but on the grand scale of things, that importance can be unimportant. Only what you really are is important.

When you meet such people you know that their apparent injustice towards you cannot hurt you if you are spiritually whole. Outward circumstances may be affected; inwardly just contact your higher force and hand over. You will be guided, you will be given strength, patience, wisdom, your path will be made smooth and straight. You need no one else in the last resort. Your own guru is inside you.

Contacting Your Higher Force

All these wonderful benefits are in store for those who choose to explore them. By meditation, whether passive or dynamic, you can put yourself in touch with your higher power and begin the life-changing and life-enhancing process I have just described.

FOUR

Mind, Meditation and Visualisation

The Mind

The first part of any practical meditation is relaxation of the body. The second stage is to learn to relax the brain, or even to bypass it, or a part of it. Our brains have two hemispheres, the left and the right. The left brain is concerned with fact and logic, the right with intuition. Ideally, the two hemispheres should work together, as they will with practice in meditation. However, when we meditate, we use our intuitive senses and the right brain takes over. The left brain, the part filled with logic, is apt to be suspicious when this happens so we need to learn to bypass it so that the right brain can take control.

The two hemispheres are the sides of the cortex of the brain. The left side, in charge of such things as logic, mathematics and science, has a 'critical censor', that is, a built-in detector of non-logic. It is this censor that the right hemisphere, largely using intuition and creative imagination, must avoid during meditation. Contrary to scientific opinion, in life one has many times to suspend judgment and accept with Shakespeare that there are 'more things in life ... than are dreamt of in your philosophy'.

Mind, as we have seen, is the real controller of the self; it is the essential 'I', the permanent personality. And it is 'I', the mind, that controls the brain and tells it what to do. If 'I' does not give it proper instructions, the brain will do all sorts of silly things on its own. If 'I' directs it, the brain will respond accordingly, particularly when it is operating at the alpha rhythm; it will allow the right hemisphere of the brain to take over from the left when necessary. And the brain in turn controls the body.

The resulting sequence then is that the body does whatever the mind wants it to do. This is why so many of us do, and become, what we don't want and don't like. People have, over time, given us the wrong feedback and we have accepted it and built on it so our brain and body act accordingly. We can literally make ourselves ill because we think we deserve it.

The Power of Positive Thinking

Suppose someone asks you how you are. You may say: 'Lousy'. Your brain takes that as a literal order, that you want to continue to feel lousy. The brain tells your body and the instruction becomes reinforced. You begin to feel worse and worse. But if you respond, 'I feel fine', then your brain–body organisation takes it as an order that you want to feel good and the better you say you feel, the better you will feel. Don't take my word for it, try it!

But can you say you feel fine if, in fact, you really feel lousy? Yes, indeed you can. Dale Carnegie claims that feeling follows action and I believe he never said a truer word. If every morning you wake and tell yourself, 'How wonderful – a new day! This is going to be a wonderful day', then it will be so. If you wake each morning dreading getting up, afraid of the day and what it will bring, then it will be a bad day for you. Truly, the power of programming yourself is tremendous. And the power of programming yourself in alpha is stunning – soon we will see how this can be achieved.

Meditation – Making the Choice

There are many ways in which you can reach the meditative state: using the relaxation response, controlling your breathing or staring into a candle flame, for example. Whichever one you choose at any particular time, these are merely techniques for 'getting you there', into the meditative state. They are not meditation per se.

I will be suggesting two methods of meditation: my whole person, deep level technique and my ABC technique. These are still only techniques to start you actually meditating. It really does not matter how you get into the meditative state in the first place, and that is why I have always looked for the simplest and quickest method of achieving this. You now know that when you are in the state of alpha, in which you experience a lower brain rhythm, you will be more aware than ever before. This is the ideal when you are meditating. There is nothing mystical about achieving that state; although some authors would have you believe that.

Once you have reached the meditative state, you have a choice. You can either sit passively and still your thoughts – I'll show you how – or you can use your brain dynamically to programme or re-programme yourself. You will do this with visualisation. A third choice could be self-hypnosis (or auto-suggestion), which really means self-instruction in alpha, but without visualisation. If you know anything about hypnosis, you will be aware that a hypnotist can assist you to go into a lower brain rhythm level (alpha or even theta) and then instruct you (brain and/or body) to respond to certain positive commands. You can do the same for yourself once you are in alpha, but generally I find the added use of visualisation is the most effective.

What Is Visualisation?

Whatever one can imagine, one can achieve! So visualisation is, in fact, imagination! The reason you must carry out your visualisation in alpha is because of the strong concentration of the brain at that level. If you can think of the brain as a circle of casually floating cells or energy units, imagine a thought moving through the brain and hitting a random number of those units. A hit-and-miss method! But in alpha, the units are concentrated together in an orderly way so that a thought goes through each one of them and therefore has a more vital and more lasting result. In alpha, you narrow the focus of your attention, whereas in beta (our normal state) you would find it much harder to get the brain to listen properly because there are too many conflicting claims on its attention.

Even in the 'waking' state after a meditative session, the energy units will remain charged and will continue to carry their dose of suggestion. Each session will reinforce previous ones and result in a build-up of constructive energy.

Being able to achieve through imagining does not mean that one could thus claim all knowledge. That would be an unrealistic assumption. For instance, a lawyer could hardly imagine himself as an electronics engineer and then expect to be one. But with this technique of visualisation in alpha, he might expect to learn more easily how to become one, if that was the way he wanted his career path to go.

The technique works because the human animal is geared to goal-seeking. Our automatic creative mechanism operates in terms of goals. Thus, if you give it a definite goal to achieve, you can depend upon your automatic guidance system to take you to that goal – much better and faster than you could ever manage by conscious thought. But the goal must be seen so clearly that it becomes real to your brain and nervous system. This is what is meant by consciously creating circumstances; it is not only possible but it is what we do all our lives. Mostly we have a bumbling, fuzzy aim at something or other, but the deliberate alpha aim is the one that works best.

No Difference Between Experience and Imagination

The concept I am describing is not really a complex one. The fact is that your automatic mechanism cannot tell the difference between an actual experience and one which is vividly imagined. The only information available to it concerning any given situation is what you believe to be true about it. And that is the whole kernel of visualisation. It is why, if we constantly picture failure to ourselves so vividly that it becomes real to our nervous system, we will be 'rewarded' with negative failure-type responses and emotions – and just the opposite when we picture ourselves as being successful and confident.

Your self-image is therefore your key to success or failure, adequacy or inadequacy. And if the image is inadequate, you must correct it, in alpha and in the dynamic meditation process.

Can Everyone Visualise?

Some people say they cannot use imagination or visualisation. When we deal with the practical techniques and the use of dynamic visualisation in Chapter 7, you will see that you can do it better than you might think. It really can work for everyone.

FIVE

All Change

Frank's Case

While many people would like to be able to change themselves, most people don't know how to go about it. Let's use Frank's story to illustrate a method for achieving change.

At the age of 35, Frank was a real mess. He was separated from his wife and young son. He was an alcoholic and in some ways a sick man. He had at times physically attacked his wife when he was drunk, but afterwards he could never remember what he had done. In this way, he was switching off responsibility for his actions. His wife had left him because she was afraid he would attack their baby son when an alcoholic spell occurred.

Frank was actually a very good salesman – he sold electric appliances and claimed to be able to sell ice to an Inuit. However, when I first saw him he was bleary-eyed and hadn't shaved for a few days. Fortunately he was off drink at that time – an interim period. He had had a domineering father and a nagging, drunken mother. At times he felt so inadequate and timid that he refused to go to work. He would take to his bed and just lie there staring at the wall or ceiling. As with so many people, these bouts of depression were the result of a constrained, inner anger. I found Frank to be a seething mass of contrary emotions, completely muddled and even at risk of a mental breakdown.

So, what could Frank do to change? First, he could stop drinking – if it were possible, and Frank thought that it was. Like so many alcoholics, he claimed: 'I can stop whenever I want. I do sometimes.'

When it was suggested that he went into an alcoholics' hospital, he snorted derisively. 'I don't need them. I'm not a true alcoholic; I don't fall into their pattern at all.' Then, after a pause, he said quietly, 'But I do know I've got to do something about myself.'

We talked for a while, particularly about his relationship with his parents. He was intelligent enough to see he had been blaming them for everything that had happened to him during his life and to realise that this just wouldn't work any more. When he had lost his father and could no longer blame him for his own problems, he had taken to another crutch, alcohol – the same one chosen by his mother.

Dependency, fear, need – all Frank's cravings and weaknesses stemmed from these negative emotions. He really had to start to rethink himself right through, to take every item that posed a query and decide whether it was right or wrong for a new Frank. To be able to list all one's bad points honestly and fearlessly is not easy, especially when one has a very small catalogue of good points to set against them. Yet each bad point has an opposite and can become its reverse, if we want to make it so.

Frank's problem was not only 'Who am I?' but also 'Where am I?' In other words, he needed to enquire why he was here at all – whether the world had any sort of meaning for him.

Frank made a detailed self-analysis and began to examine the positive and negative points in his character. He drew up a list, which he headed with this note:

'This list is only for me so I can be as caustic or as sanctimonious as I like. And if my outreach is too high it's the fault of my counsellor, but I'm glad he's made me do it. Here is my "Balance Sheet":'

Assets

Good physical health

Feel confident at times, although perhaps a false confidence

Generous at times

Can love, although not really able to love another fully

Liabilities

Poor mental health

Depression

Periodical craving for alcohol

Feel inferior more often than not; hide this under aggression

Selfish

Need praise, approval

Despise weak people (am I afraid of looking into a mirror?)

Paternalistic really, and only kind when I can 'afford' to be so generous

Boastful

Sometimes greedy

'Hard' in business

Want my own way

Impatient

Afraid as hell of almost everything, and afraid of showing it

Get very angry when thwarted or challenged; overbearing

Afraid to trust, to let go

Enjoy sex at times (though not at all when drunk) but as a pleasure for myself; not very concerned about my partner

Strategy or goal to be adopted

I can accept that I tend towards alcoholism and I shall join AA. All the above negative traits must be turned to positive ones.

Relationships

With parents

Hated my old man but was afraid of him and obeyed him. My mother nagged me to distraction. She was afraid of him too, hence her drinking. I wasn't all that kind to her. Both are dead now. I realise there's no use regretting the past. The best I can do for anything I've done wrong is to do better in the future.

With those at work

We're strictly in competition. It's always been either them or me and I never let it be them – I've always put myself first. I shall try to visualise myself acting in different ways. We'll see if consideration for others pays off in satisfaction; I can take that risk.

Questions about work: What have I really been doing there? What would I really like to do there? What do I want to become?

With customers

I've always given good service because I know it pays best. But it's not from feelings of goodwill or caring. If I'm doing a good job, I could do an even better one with concern for the customers' real needs.

With family

When I read through my liabilities I can see what my wife has had to put up with. Do I want her back or would I rather start afresh? Would starting afresh help? She stuck with me in the bad days and we could have a good life if I can really change myself. And the boy – we must give him a good home; I think we owe him that. So yes, I do want her back, and on her terms.

General action to be taken

I've got a few decent instincts but I always smother them when I feel them emerging, on the basis of: 'I have to look after No. 1 first'. If I can acquire more self-confidence, not just on the surface but really deep inside, then I won't have to be afraid of what other people think or say or do. I don't have to be in competition all the time, just do the best I can. Then I wouldn't have to be afraid of not getting or having things or the approval of others. And if people challenge me it won't really matter because I will know what's true or not. Nor does it really matter what others think of me – that's their business. If I do my best for my family and myself, and for others, then I can't do more. I can see that now. And if I can get and keep that inner peace, then I won't have anything to get angry about.

I've got the technique now on how to work on myself and things are starting to change. I do want to change – not to become saintly (joke!) but to be in control, to be my real inner self.

The Secret of Change

To simplify this to the utmost: if you're unhappy, find out what is wrong – and change it.

Too simple? Not really. Just go one step at a time into visualisation through alpha. Work on one item at a time – say for a week at a time – and see the changes developing. Anyone can change if they want to work at it – say two quarter-hour sessions a day. It isn't very onerous and it really can work if you give it a chance.

You can't achieve this kind of change by will-power, only by using your imagination and belief. What the mind can conceive and you can believe – you can achieve. But if will and imagination come into conflict, imagination wins every time. To illustrate: try not to think of two very large lions for five minutes …

Self-analysis

Do you recall the case of Kathy in Chapter 1? Her problem was finding her real identity. She needed constant approval and she had to learn how to control her emotions. Well, she made her self-analysis and then she decided exactly what kind of person she wanted to be. Through visualisation in alpha she learnt to watch herself in various circumstances, and then she would replay the scenes as she would like them to have taken place. In this way she conditioned herself to changing her attitudes, her feelings and her actions. She said it was like restructuring or remoulding herself. She literally made herself over, so that she was the same person but different in several important ways.

A useful way to start self-analysis is to record for a few days your reactions to people and events. First, make a list of all the negative qualities you can think of, such as fearfulness, anger, jealousy, resentment, pride, irritability, self-pity, hatred, criticising, judging – just as Frank did. Then make a parallel list of positive qualities you already possess but want to develop, and qualities which you do not have but would like to see as part of your make-up.

Then when any unpleasant incident occurs, you must note your reaction to it and identify which one of those negative qualities has come into play. Then ask yourself why you reacted in that way. If you're being honest – and you must be scrupulously honest – you'll soon get a true picture of yourself. Whatever other people say or do, they are not responsible for your actions or reactions – you are. If you are not happy with those reactions, you can change them whenever you wish.

It is usually our strong ego that makes us act negatively, and when we realise this we can prepare ourselves to react differently in the future. One example would be reacting with anger, or with self-pity, against another's anger. If we regularly react angrily when presented with someone else's anger, it can become a habit, a daily state of affairs. Whatever that does to the other person, it can certainly not be good for us, as we will experience the negative effects of anger over and over again. If we begin to realise that and distance ourselves from it, we can learn to observe the other person's anger and perhaps even discover just why they are angry, but we will have no need to react to it with our own anger.

This was certainly the case with Frank, although he had even more problems. His main one was how to acquire more self-confidence so that he could become the sort of person he'd really like to be. If he could believe in himself, he would have no need to rely on alcohol to give him that false confidence he had been leaning on. He also needed to learn how to handle his anger. He worked on controlling his drinking, and in due course gave it up altogether.

What he did to build his self-confidence was not only to replay his scenes, as Kathy did, but also to play out scenes in his imagination in advance of their happening. Mentally and visually, he scheduled contacts with people, including his wife, as he wanted these to be. He would visualise himself acting out scenarios with other people in which he was in control of himself. Mentally, he would draw up scripts for how each confrontation would turn out so that when he actually came face to face with these people, the scenes turned out much as he'd planned. He geared himself and his behaviour for optimum response and he got it. Gradually, he began to see that he could actually make things happen in a positive way. He began to succeed!

Re-programming Yourself

Can an angry person – someone who gets angry all the time – stop being angry once they discover that it is literally poisoning their system and their relationships?

The point is that reason very seldom comes into the question of anger; it is emotion gone haywire, out of control. The yogi adage says: 'An ignorant man becomes angry; the wise man understands.' The wise man is someone who understands himself first and, therefore, understands others.

When we snap back at others, it is our touchy ego-self that makes us do it. But if we are calm inside we understand what is going on and so don't hit out. Now in order for the angry person to be able to achieve this state, they must first re-programme themselves.

Let us assume that you have been through your own personal self-analysis and will therefore know which items you want to re-programme. You will have started this process by looking at your self-image. In most people this has become set by the age of about six. Sounds a bit young, doesn't it? But it is so. If you have ever watched youngsters grow up you can see that basically they remain the same people they always were. Your good points are reinforced but so are your bad ones (which is why no one should ever marry another with the thought that bad behaviour will miraculously improve; it will only worsen with familiarity). The truth is that everyone suffers from an inadequate self-image in some aspect or another.

The reason is that we all feel ineffective in certain areas and we believe we always will. In those areas we have fixated our bad points instead of trying to change them. As far as these are concerned we have literally programmed ourselves (usually with outside critical help) for negativity and failure.

When I look back at my own experience, I was patterned in shyness, a lack of self-confidence which had probably arisen from a severe hand and face injury – I was burnt under a mosquito net when I was tiny. When I had a job which at times demanded a certain amount of extroversion, I forced myself to take a public-speaking course. I made myself mix freely with people, but it was a struggle.

Self-confidence, or the lack of it, is a good example for us because it applies to so many people. Often it is created by parents who unwittingly make a child feel small and inadequate.'You're such a fool,' shouts the father. Or: 'Why are you such a clumsy boy? Useless, aren't you?'

Of course, there are many other ways it can come about, but in any event over the years the negativity is reinforced by other incidents. Is it any wonder people become ineffective, or perhaps tries to make themselves seem better by scoring off other people? I'm sure we all know many people who try to cover up their inadequacy in that way.

Frederick Bailes, an author on healing through science of the mind techniques, claims that timid or shy people are usually so because of unconscious hostility through low self-esteem. Such people may feel that others are against them, that for instance they will be criticised if they do not talk as well as others. This keeps them silent. It also makes them poor salesmen. It also makes them too introverted and separates them from others. In a sense it is self-centredness because they are constantly thinking of themselves, the impression they are making, the possible criticisms of others. They are afraid of being hurt. Their love is going inwards and not outwards. What they need is to shift their centre of attention towards others, ready to give of themself whatever the outcome.

Whatever the cause, that person knows their own inadequacy – their inadequate self-image – and now they must deliberately set out to change that self-image to the one of their own choice. What they need to do is to 'see' the bad picture of themselves – as they are, or as they have been up to that point. Then they must cancel it and follow it with the good picture of the new person they want to be. If they continue to do this every day for at least a week, the new programming will eventually 'set'. This is how visualisation works. It is not a new theory and it can be found in any number of books. What is crucial to visualisation is that it must be done in the alpha state. When people fail to achieve life changes through visualisation, this happens because they have not done it in alpha.

This is dynamic meditation in use. To sum up, our aim is to de-programme and then re-programme ourselves. We have first accepted that everyone is the architect of their own future, that we are what we choose to be. By everything we do each day, we create what is to come later. You have to forget the past. There is no use having guilty feelings, for what is done is done. If you can make amends – well and good. Do it, then forget and forgive yourself. In other words, accept yourself as you are now and as you intend to become. Realise that past possibilities no longer exist, only future ones. You are going to create your new self-image as you desire to be.

You may have heard the saying 'To change what you get, you must change what you are.' Remember that everything that exists physically has existed first in thought. Even such a mundane thing as a cake! So if we don't like the experience we have, we have to change the kind of thoughts we have. Changing our thought pattern will change our behaviour – and that in turn will change our future experiences.

We must therefore plan ourselves, our mental attitudes and a whole improved personal world; we must create the right sort of goals and make a bee-line for them.

The Need for Goals

Everyone needs goals in life; things they want to achieve. They do not have to be huge goals – to change the world, to conquer the stars –

they can be as basic or simple as you like. They might be to find a part-time job, to do some social work, to work for oneself, to be a better husband or wife – whatever suits your circumstances. If you feel you do not have any goals in life, set yourself a small and realistic target to aim for.

Even a small daily goal will do as a start – no need for any special traits or strengths. Everyone has something – some way of living more interestingly, of helping others. You only have to take one objective at a time, and realise that there's as much pleasure and satisfaction in the doing as in the achieving. The trying is just as important as the eventual success. The actual doing is what brings inner contentment. And if all is well now, then that immediately frees you from tomorrow's demands.

Times of trauma and crisis in life – when you are grieving over a loss, for example – are times when you are more than ever vulnerable to mental stress or physical illness. These are times perhaps to revise your goals. Set smaller targets so that you can work towards them, for example: 'Tomorrow I will think of five good memories of the person I have lost.' Work towards that goal, then re-establish another when you have achieved it. This will help you move on, for one thing which is certain in life is change.

As we set our personal goals, we can think about our greatest needs: self-acceptance, self-esteem, self-appreciation and self-celebration, a feeling of joy in ourselves, a bubbling-over because we are who we are – just because we are here and alive and experiencing life. We aim to experience none of these things in a self-satisfied, smug way, but just in a glad feeling of being ourselves, of having been chosen to be as we are. When we can feel that, we are able to offer love freely and unconditionally to others. Once we can rejoice in ourselves, we can rejoice in others as well.

A *Permanent High*

Might this feeling be a possible result of reaching our goals, actually achieving our needs? Perhaps – and why not? Isn't that life's true potential, perhaps – to be on a permanent high? If we are in tune, unafraid, loving, open to life and expecting the best, who could want more? Not even the greediest people, since if they felt loving and in tune they wouldn't be greedy any longer.

The psychologist Erich Fromm called greed a bottomless pit which exhausts the person in an endless effort to satisfy his needs without ever reaching satisfaction. Greedy people, he said, are always anxiously concerned with themselves. They are never satisfied, always restless, driven by the fear of not getting enough, of missing something, of being deprived of something. They are filled with burning envy of anyone who might have more than them. Basically, they are people who are not fond of themselves at all but, on the contrary, deeply dislike themselves.

Sai Baba, the Indian guru, recounts the following peculiar method of trapping monkeys in India and uses it as an example to teach about human greed and desire:

> 'The process consists of bringing a big pot with a small mouth and keeping some material which is attractive to the monkeys inside the pot. A monkey takes a handful of the material and cannot then pull its hand out. It imagines that someone inside the pot is gripping its hand. The monkey has trapped itself because it has taken in its hand such a lot of material. The moment it lets go of the material, it could be free. Man binds himself in the same way by grasping and being unable to let go.'

Greed and competitiveness go in concert and competition is related closely to envy and jealousy, insecurity, anxiety and distrust of those around. But a contented person is, therefore, without greed.

SIX

The Deep Level and ABC
Ultimate Techniques

Relaxation Techniques

Before we look at meditation techniques, let's look at some ways of relaxing physically. They may not be enough on their own to defeat all those potentially nasty things stress can do to you but, practised regularly, they will help to restore your vigour, and there are plenty of methods you can employ. You simply have to find one that works for you. Later, we'll go on to the ABC technique, which automatically relaxes both body and brain and can bring you the deeper benefits obtained by meditation or self-hypnosis.

To relax physically, some people simply drop on to the floor or on to a bed like a leaf and lie there on their back, legs slightly apart and arms loosely by their sides. This is a simple way of relaxing, especially after indulging in physical activity, be it hard physical work or sports.

Others need a different technique, and if you find that you cannot relax physically because your mind is still racing, try visualising yourself as a floating piece of seaweed drifting with the tide. This can help, and you may doze off for a few minutes and wake up feeling physically restored and less tense.

Again, however, many people find that they cannot simply 'switch off', and for them the best method to use is generally a form of progressive relaxation, quickly tensing and relaxing every muscle in the body. Because it follows a specific technique and the brain is concentrating on the body, it is very effective for most people.

To achieve progessive relaxation, start by sitting upright but comfortably in an armchair so that every part of your body is adequately supported, then breathe very deeply in and out a few times to calm the body. Close your eyes and concentrate on your body, one set of muscles at a time.

First, put your toes together, pigeon-toed, heels a little apart, and push your toes down into the floor to tighten and tense the muscles in your feet and lower legs. Next, tighten your thighs, then your buttocks. Tighten your abdomen, trying to press it against the small of your back. Tense your shoulder muscles and the muscles in your chest. Raise your arms, fists clenched and elbows stiff. Squeeze your eyes tightly shut and clench your teeth. Keeping your face tight and screwed up, arch your neck and point your chin up. Although this may sound a bit long-winded, it should only take about 30 seconds. Finally, hold your breath and hold that feeling of tension right through your body for about seven seconds.

Then relax completely and feel all that tension flow out of you. Drop your chin down and let your arms fall back to your sides. Concentrate for a few seconds on feeling all the tension flowing out. Check through the muscles of the toes, legs and thighs. If there is still any tension there, release it, just let it go. Relax the muscles of your abdomen and back, the muscles of your shoulders, arms and fingers – let them all feel nice and heavy – and the muscles of your face, your jaw, your eyelids, even your scalp.

Take a deep breath and hold it for a few seconds, then let it out slowly and say silently to yourself, 'Relax, relax'. Think about the difference in the way you felt when your muscles were tense and when you relaxed. Say to yourself: 'Whenever I instruct myself to relax, this is how I will feel.'

After a while, with daily practice, you will simply be able to say, 'relax, relax', and your body will automatically do everything for you. Don't be in a rush to achieve this; use the process regularly and eventually you will gain control.

Use the step-by-step reminder on page 64 if you need to while you are practising the technique. I still use this method of physical relaxation as the starting point for meditation, and it is appropriate whichever meditation technique you use. My two meditation techniques are both discussed later in the book.

Meditation Techniques

As I have mentioned, I have developed and tested two techniques to take you into an alpha state ready for meditation: the whole person, deep level technique and the ABC ultimate technique, which I believe is the fastest and easiest. The deep level technique is the one I devised first, and I am going to explain the process in case you prefer that technique to the faster method. You may find it takes slightly longer to learn and master. However, some will prefer one method and some the other; simply choose what is best for you.

For the whole person technique, you will need to relax your body before you begin to relax your brain. I described the technique for this on page 62. In the ABC technique, you won't need this deliberate relaxation since the whole system slips quickly into gear. I use that word deliberately because it really is rather like using an automatic gear-change on a car instead of a manual one.

Whichever method you choose, what you do need until you become adept is a quiet place where you can be uninterrupted. It is best to meditate regularly because there is then a cumulative effect for good. And if you are working on a specific problem, the best results will come from meditating at least twice a day for about 15 minutes.

Once you have mastered the technique of your choice, you will be able to meditate anywhere, at any time – on a bus or train or even standing up – to work on your problems or just if you need a few seconds' quiet.

Progressive Physical Relaxation

This summary of the technique is designed to help you practise physical relaxation and supports the full information in the text.

- *Sit comfortably with your whole body supported.*
- *Breathe in and out deeply a few times.*
- *Close your eyes.*
- *Push your toes into the floor and tense the muscles in your feet and lower legs.*
- *Tighten your thighs.*
- *Tighten your buttocks.*
- *Tighten your abdomen.*
- *Tense your shoulder and chest muscles.*
- *Raise your arms, tighten your arm muscles and clench your fists.*
- *Squeeze your eyes tightly shut and clench your teeth.*
- *Arch your neck and point your chin up.*
- *Hold your breath for seven seconds.*
- *Breathe out deeply.*
- *Relax completely and feel the tension flow out of you.*
- *Check through your body that all tension has been released.*
- *Take a deep breath and hold it for a few seconds.*
- *Breathe out deeply.*
- *Tell yourself: 'Relax, relax'.*
- *Tell yourself: 'Whenever I instruct myself to relax, this is how I will feel.'*

Your Serene Scene

Whichever of the following techniques you use for meditation, I will teach you to achieve a deeper level of consciousness, the level of alpha. Once you have done this, you will step into an imaginary place which is special to you – the place where you will meditate – so I will talk about this place first as it applies equally to both techniques.

As we have already explained, you must learn to evade the critical censor in your left brain. You can do this by creating for yourself a special place to go – in your imagination – which we will call your 'serene scene'.

Your serene scene can be any place chosen by you. It is usually a natural scene, but it could be any private place of relaxation. Perhaps it will be a place that you have enjoyed visiting and where you have felt at peace. Alternatively, it could be a place you have always wanted to visit. It may be a peaceful garden or meadow, somewhere you find particularly soothing, or possibly a quiet beach by the sea. But, wherever it is, when you go there in your imagination make every detail of your scene so real that you can see the individual blades of grass, the petals on the flowers; or see and feel the sand under your feet. Feel the warmth of the sun, the coolness and softness of the grass. Hear the gentle swish and lapping of the sea, a breeze rustling through the trees. Envision the blue sky with small white clouds here and there. If there is a pond or stream, take a look at it. Let your mind take you there and really be there!

Some people claim that they have no imagination and cannot picture things in this kind of detail, but this is not really true. They simply need to practise to confirm and develop their ability to imagine.

If you feel you are in this category, close your eyes and go in your imagination to a refrigerator. Open the door and take a lemon out of the fridge. It feels cold in your hand. Look closely at it. Squeeze it and feel how firm it is. Now, in your mind, go to the kitchen drawer and take out a knife. Cut the lemon in two. Smell it. Bite it and let some of the juice fall on your tongue. Ten to one your mouth will be watering. Your body says: 'I'm biting a lemon. It's sour so I must salivate and wash the juice away.'

Well, you see, you told your brain you were eating a lemon. Your brain accepted the instruction and went to work with the body. The brain is not a subtle interpreter; it accepts what it is told.

Go through this scenario until you can imagine different fruits; feel your success. Then move on to develop your serene scene.

The Whole Person, Deep Level Technique

This is how you use the whole person, deep level technique.

The first thing to do is to relax your body, as described on pages 62–3. Sit comfortably in an armchair, as upright as you can, with your lower back leaning into the chair and every part of your body supported. Start with this position and experiment with what suits you best. As long as you are able completely to relax your body, position is not actually important.

Once you have relaxed your body, you need to relax your brain by moving to a deeper level of consciousness, the level of alpha. In this technique, I teach people to count themselves down to that deep level, and you can follow the step-by-step instructions to achieve that.

Some people prefer to use an imaginary escalator or a lift (elevator), but generally I have found my way to be better. One particular pupil preferred to go up rather than down, which only shows how malleable the imagination can be. Try my way first, then develop your own. It is all about your own success in achieving the alpha level.

I will now run through the instructions as though I am addressing you directly, but when you have got the hang of it you will be able to instruct yourself mentally in the same way, in your own words. A good way to do it to start with is to record the instructions on a tape recorder. Strangely, this plays back to you almost as though it is not your own voice at all. Speak the instructions slowly, but firmly and rather monotonously and it will play back as though someone else is instructing you.

You have your body relaxed and it is feeling completely free of tension and at peace. Breathe in and out deeply a few times.

Now I want you to visualise (with your eyes closed) being in a large room. It is a busy room and there is a hum of noise.

You wish to be quiet so you move towards the back of the room, towards a smaller room where the connecting door is open. You go in there and close the door behind you, shutting yourself off from the other, larger room.

Now all is suddenly peaceful and you see a chair there, a comfortable chair, and you sink into it knowing that you are going to move down, down, inside yourself to a place where you will be completely relaxed, both physically and mentally.

When I tell you, you will press a button, which is on the arm of the chair, and I will count you down – in your chair – from ten to zero and you will then see yourself moving down, deeper and deeper, until at zero you will reach a deep level and then you will, in your mind, stand up and step out into your serene scene.

All right. Press your button now and start moving down, in your chair, as I count you down from ten to zero. And each time I say a number or the word 'deeper', you will go ten times deeper.

Ten ... Nine ... Deeper and deeper ... Eight ... Deeper still, down, down ... Seven ... Deeper and deeper ... Six ... Five ... Feel yourself going deeper, moving down ... Four ... Go deeper ... Three ... Deeper and deeper ... Two ... One ... Zero.

You are now at a deeper inner level of consciousness and feeling completely relaxed. And now, in your mind, you stand up and move into your serene scene. And each time you come here you will be at a still deeper level.

This is the whole person, deep level technique for going into alpha.

The Whole Person, Deep Level Technique

This summary of the technique is designed to help you practise going into a meditative state and supports the full information in the text. As you develop your technique, you will gradually personalise your own approach.

- *Sit comfortably and relax your body (see page 64).*
- *Breathe in and out deeply two or three times.*
- *Visualise yourself in a busy room.*
- *Move towards a connecting door at the back of the room.*
- *Go through into a smaller, quiet room and close the door behind you.*
- *The room is calm and peaceful.*
- *Sit down on the comfortable chair.*
- *Tell yourself that you are going to move down inside yourself to a place where you will be completely relaxed, physically and mentally.*
- *Press the button on the arm of the chair.*
- *Count yourself down from ten to zero, moving deeper at each count.*
- *At the alpha level, stand up and move into your serene scene.*
- *Sit down on your comfortable chair and be ready to meditate.*

ABC: *The Ultimate Technique*

Let us now look at the ABC technique and then we can discuss what happens in meditation once the technique has taken us there.

As I said before, once you have mastered your chosen technique, you can meditate anywhere, but to begin with sit quietly in a chair that comfortably supports your spine. The reason I call this the ABC technique, apart from the fact that it is so quick and simple, is that it has three steps:

Step 1: 'A' stands for 'Above' (or looking upwards, as you will see in a moment).

Step 2: 'B' stands for 'Be closed'.

Step 3: 'C' stands for 'Ceal' (a free version of 'seal').

Step 1: Breathe deeply two or three times, in and out. Now stare at a point in front of you above your eye level but without raising your head. Say mentally: 'A', knowing this is the first step of three. As you repeat the 'A' you will soon feel your eyes tiring or stinging a little. As you stare, keep saying to yourself: 'A – my eyelids are getting heavy; I will soon want to close my eyes.'

Step 2: As soon as you feel you'd like to close your eyes, do so and say: 'B – Be closed. My eyelids want to stay closed. They are heavy and want to stay closed.' Feel their heaviness.

The secret is that, as in hypnosis and self-hypnosis, total relaxation of the entire body starts with the closing of the eyes and, importantly, the relaxation of the upper eyelids. Your body cannot remain tense when your eyelids are relaxed properly. When you 'stare' in Step 1, this is done in order to tire the upper eyelid muscles.

Step 3: Now say to yourself: 'C – Ceal' and imagine that your closed eyelids are being sealed together with a pleasant, soothing but very sticky and secure (though completely harmless) glue or sealant. Feel that your eyelids are so firmly sealed together that you know it would take a real effort to open your eyes. Don't press your lids tightly together because then you will be introducing tension. Just feel them gummed together but perfectly relaxed.

Your eyelids are now fully relaxed. Let yourself feel this relaxation slowly move down your face, your cheeks, your jaw, then down your neck and shoulders and slowly right down your body to your feet. While doing this relaxation, simultaneously take a deep breath and slowly let it out and feel it flowing right down through your body to your feet. If you run out of breath, take a second one.

After a little practice this whole procedure will probably take about 15 seconds, maybe less.

At first I suggest you now say: 'I am going deeper still.' Then mentally count yourself slowly down from five to zero, like this: 'Five ... Four ... Deeper and deeper ... Three ... Two ... Deeper still ... One ... Zero. I am now at a deep level.' This can be repeated again if you wish. You will now almost certainly be in alpha. Each time you meditate, tell yourself that every time you come to your serene scene you will be at a much deeper level than before.

Your aim in this exercise has been to reach a place called 'deep level' where you will be able to step mentally into your serene scene. You will recall that this is a remembered or imagined place where you feel happy and peaceful, perhaps a garden or a beach. Return to the same place mentally each time you meditate, so it becomes easy and familiar.

Now visualise yourself stepping into your serene scene and then sitting down in a comfortable chair. You have come here either to meditate passively or to work on yourself. We will talk about both these techniques in the next chapter and explain how meditation works.

The ABC Ultimate Technique

This summary of the technique is designed to help you practise going into a meditative state and supports the full information in the text. As you develop your technique, you will gradually personalise your own approach.

- *Sit comfortably and relax your body (see page 64).*
- *Breathe in and out deeply two or three times.*
- *Stare at a point in front of you above eye level and say to yourself 'A'.*
- *Keep repeating to yourself: 'My eyelids are getting heavy; I will soon want to close my eyes.'*
- *As soon as you want to close your eyes, do so and say to yourself 'B'.*
- *Keep repeating to yourself: 'My eyelids are heavy and want to stay closed.'*
- *Say to yourself 'C'.*
- *Feel your eyelids so firmly sealed that it would take a real effort to open your eyes.*
- *Feel your eyelids fully relaxed.*
- *Let that relaxation slowly move down your face, cheeks and jaw.*
- *Feel the relaxation move down your neck and shoulders.*
- *Feel the relaxation travel down the rest of your body to your feet.*
- *Take one or two deep breaths as you do this.*
- *Mentally count yourself down from five to zero, moving deeper at each count.*
- *At the alpha level, stand up and move into your serene scene.*
- *Sit down on your comfortable chair and be ready to meditate.*

Feeling Sleepy

You should not feel yourself becoming sleepy while in alpha, but if this does happen, shake your head from side to side for a moment and it will clear.

However, if you want to use alpha for going to sleep at night, go down into the alpha state, and then count yourself deeper and deeper. Tell yourself, 'Let go, let go', and then instruct yourself that you are now in self-hypnosis and will simply drift into normal sleep – and you will.

Counting Yourself Up

To complete the process, you need a technique to restore you to your normal, working level of consciousness, your beta level.

Restoring your brain to its normal rhythms after you have been to your deep level for meditation is quite simple. I will explain it here so that the entry and exit processes are complete, but you would normally count yourself up after meditating.

Once you have finished your meditation (as described in the next chaper), tell yourself, in your own words: 'I shall now count myself up from one to five and at five I shall open my eyes and feel better, fitter and stronger than before, alert and refreshed and full of energy.' Then count slowly from one to five; at three, move your fingers and toes, and at five, open your eyes.

Counting Yourself Up Technique

This summary of the technique is designed to help you practise counting yourself up and supports the full information in the text. As you develop your technique, you will gradually personalise your own approach.

- *Complete your meditation.*

- *Tell yourself: 'I shall now count myself up from one to five.'*

- *Tell yourself: 'At five, I shall open my eyes and feel better, fitter and stronger than before, alert and refreshed and full of energy.'*

- *Count 'one ... two' to yourself and feel yourself rising from the deep level.*

- *Count 'three' to yourself, feel yourself rising further and move your fingers and toes.*

- *Count 'four' to yourself and feel yourself rising further.*

- *Count 'five' to yourself and open your eyes.*

- *Confirm the feeling of metal and physical relaxation you have achieved.*

Fast Tension Relief

Once you have learnt the ABC technique, you can use it in almost any circumstances and wherever you happen to be as an instant 'refresher'. With practice you will only need to close your eyes and sweep the feeling of relaxation from your eyes right down your body, remain in that state for a minute or even less, then tell yourself that when you open your eyes you will feel fully refreshed, alert and full of energy.

For really instant alpha, you can later instruct yourself – while at your deep level – that whenever you touch your thumb to your third or ring finger and say to yourself 'deep level' you will immediately go there. Do it, practise it, and it will work.

SEVEN

Meditation at Work

What Is Meditation?

What is the feeling you achieve during meditation? It is hard to answer
that question since we probably do not all experience it in quite the
same way. It seems to me to be experienced at the back of the skull.
When we move from the beta to the alpha brain-rhythm level, our
consciousness seems to move downwards from the top of our heads
until it reaches the alpha level near the base of the head. The feeling
is almost analogous to changing gear in a car. As our brain rhythm
shifts down to a slower, calmer level, it feels just like a shift in the
power of a car's engine.

My personal belief is that when we reach alpha and want to go to a
still deeper state, theta, the mind starts to expand outwards so that it
moves from the more confined space of awareness within the skull to
embrace the consciousness that is outside the physical body.

In fact, I believe that the mind can reach out to the consciousness that
is part of everything and everyone. This deep state is not really needed

for working dynamically on oneself, however. The alpha level is sufficient for that.

Dynamic Meditation

After you have gone into alpha and your serene scene, you then have the option of using either passive or dynamic meditation, or first one and then the other. Since I usually use dynamic meditation first and finish off with passive meditation, I will deal with them in that order.

Dynamic meditation, as we have already said, is about changing yourself: changing bad habits, de-programming and re-programming yourself to make yourself as you want to be and can become. It can mean improving your health, changing your outlook, changing the way you deal with people, and so on.

You have relaxed both body and mind and moved down to the alpha level of consciousness. You are now sitting on a chair – or on the grass or beach or whatever – in your serene scene. You are enjoying being there, seeing the softness and cool greenness of the grass, feeling the gentle warmth of the sun, hearing the slight breeze rustling through the trees. You can see the blue sky with small clouds here and there. Just sit for a few moments and feel how relaxed you are and how much you are at peace there.

You recognise that you are now at a much deeper and more inward level of mind, near to the very source of your being. Tell yourself you are now completely relaxed in body and brain and that whenever you instruct yourself to relax, this is how you will feel and at the same time you will become more aware and alert at your inner conscious levels. Remind yourself that you, yourself, are always in full control.

I want you now to repeat to yourself, in your mind, one or more positive phrases of this sort for your own benefit:

'From now on I shall be continually thinking positive thoughts that will make me successful, happy, well and prosperous.'

'I will be able to use more and more of my mind, and in such a special way that I will have full and complete control over my senses and faculties at every level of the mind.'

'From now on my body and my life are free from all disturbing influences. I am at peace.'

'I have all the strength I need to do whatever I have to do, and all ways are open to me.'

'There is peace, harmony and freedom in every situation and in every person with whom I come into contact.'

'I will be using my positive thinking to bring me the understanding and awareness that I desire, so that my improved mental faculties may be used for the good of myself and others, and to serve humanity better.'

A Mind Screen

Facing you now in your serene scene is a large screen, rather like a cinema screen. It is a mental screen on which much of your work on yourself will be done while you are at your deep level.

The reason for using the mind screen is as follows. If you sit in your serene scene and 'see' yourself there in your mind, it is at its most effective if you can really be there in your imagination, seeing and feeling the grass, the flowers, the blue sky, the breeze, the sun. Then if you focus on to an imagined screen and you see yourself on that screen, since the screen image is twice removed from the actual you sitting in your room, that imagined situation somehow becomes a more real situation to your brain. And indeed it is a more focused one than simply visualising and working on yourself. But if you have a preference for one method over another, use it.

You now see your mind screen lit up. The first time you try out this technique, project an apple, rather larger than life size, on to the screen. Blow it up in size so that it becomes quite big. Make it three-dimensional so that you can see all around it. Examine its colour, its stalk and the markings on the skin. Have it turn around so that you can see the back of it and look at it clearly and closely for a few seconds. Take a little time to become really acquainted with your apple. If you prefer, you can use a banana or an orange, or a flower for that matter. It is the exercise in visualisation that is important.

Now while you are sitting there in your serene scene, I want you, in your mind, to look down on your lap and see a small electronic control, like a small box with two knobs on it. When you press the first, a picture will appear on the screen, whatever picture you want. The second knob, when pressed, will destroy your picture when it needs to be changed. I call this 'automatic destruct'.

Remember, knob one gives you a new picture and knob two is automatic destruct.

Let's see how this works. Suppose you want to change a bad habit. Come to your deep level, sit down in your serene scene opposite your mind screen, light it up and see a picture of yourself as you really are. Tell yourself you are going to change this.

Next, press the second knob, on the right, and the picture will disintegrate.

Press the first knob again and see a new picture of yourself as you intend to be. Tell yourself this is how it will be.

The pictures do not have to be static ones. You can envisage yourself as though in a movie if you wish.

You will be able to use this technique for almost anything. For instance, you can use it if you suffer from nerves when speaking to people or when making a speech. You would first picture yourself being tongue-tied, worrying how you will sound or forgetting what you have to say. Always make this first picture a little worse than it really is – exaggerate it. Then destroy it and change the picture to how you want it to be and how it will become. For example, in making a speech, you would see yourself talking easily and in a relaxed way as if you were by yourself or with a close but slightly deaf friend. Then this is how it will happen. Don't forget that you must always first visualise the condition you wish to change.

When you greatly desire something to happen, believe that it will, and expect it to happen. Those are three magic words: Desire, Believe, Expect – DBE!

Dynamic Meditation Technique

This summary of the technique is designed to help you practise your own meditation technique and supports the full information in the text. As you develop your technique, you will gradually personalise your own approach.

- *Sit comfortably and relax your body (see page 64).*
- *Breathe in and out deeply two or three times.*
- *Move down to the alpha level.*
- *At the alpha level, stand up and move into your serene scene.*
- *Sit down on your comfortable chair and be ready to meditate.*
- *Sit comfortably in your serene scene and feel relaxed and at peace.*
- *Experience the sensations of your serene scene.*
- *Repeat your positive phrases.*
- *Light up your mind screen.*
- *Press the first button on your control panel.*
- *Project your first, negative picture on to the mind screen and experience the scene.*
- *Press the second button on your control panel.*
- *See the image disintegrate.*
- *Project the positive image on to the mind screen and experience the scene.*
- *Complete your meditation.*
- *Count yourself up to beta levels.*

You see, if you desire some attribute, some way of doing things – even something material you need in your life – but believe and expect it will not and cannot happen, then it never will. But when you believe it can, expect that it will and actually see it happening on your screen, then you start off a chain of changing circumstances that will create whatever you want. This is true and you can accept this truth, knowing that it is indeed so.

This technique can be used to change yourself in any way you wish. We will talk about health later on. But if you want to change anything about yourself – smoking, drinking, the way you work, getting more confidence, playing sport, your attitude to life or to people – you will simply go to your deep level and switch on your mind screen and see yourself doing what you don't like, or behaving in any way you'd like to change. Tell yourself that you don't like it, that in fact you will simply not have it so. Then destroy that image and finally see yourself, the new you, being as you wish to be, acting as you would wish, as you've always wanted. Do this twice a day and you will soon become the person in the new picture.

When you have finished your meditation, count yourself back up to your normal beta levels (see page 73) and you will feel energised and totally refreshed.

Deciding One's Own Destiny

Experience has proved that this method of changing how you are really does work. Even if you believe in fate to a limited extent – in other words that our guidelines are laid out for us but that we can fill in the in-betweens for ourselves – we can still make a difference. We can plan our goals and make ourselves into the kind of people we want to be. Is that not deciding one's own destiny?

When you find that your past image has in some way been inadequate, correct it. Imagine yourself, on your screen, as already being the kind of person you wish to be. If, for instance, you are a fearful and over-anxious person, you will see yourself acting calmly, confidently and with courage. Then you will become what you see. If you recall bad scenarios when you wish you had acted differently to the way you did, re-enact them as you would like them to have occurred. You can't change what another person said or did, but you can correct the way you acted and that would possibly have changed the way the other person behaved. You cannot change how other people feel or behave, but your actions will influence what they decide to do in any given circumstance.

Suppose you are a writer. If you have any hang-ups about writing, this is the place to get rid of them. The same goes for improving music-playing, acting, painting, playing tennis or golf. For ball games, for example, watch yourself smoothly dealing with the ball, shot by shot. But you must do it in detail – a short movie for this, not just a snapshot. You need to see the perfect contact with the ball, the good feeling of your muscles as you do it, the follow-through, the ball moving exactly to its target, time after time, and people congratulating you after a performance. Did you know that Ben Hogan played every golf stroke in his mind before he made the shot? The renowned Beethoven pianist Artur Schnabel practised even more in his mind than at the piano. Many other successful people have found that working in the mind provides one of the best methods of achievement.

The field is unlimited. Suppose you have a fear of flying. Go into alpha – deep level, serene scene – then visualise yourself on your mind screen facing a journey and feeling your usual fear. Next, destroy that picture and then visualise yourself making a safe, smooth and enjoyable trip. See yourself actually sitting in comfort, listening to the usual sounds in a plane, looking out and noticing beautiful cloud formations, feeling relaxed and rested. At the same time, give yourself positive verbal messages. Repeat this procedure over and over for a couple of weeks, and by then your automatic system will have absorbed the changed message.

Contacting Your Subconscious

Let us look a little more closely at smoking, drinking, losing weight – if these are things you want to change in your lifestyle. First you must never forget that you may subconsciously want to keep doing the very thing you consciously seem to want to get rid of. Your subconscious may have adopted it as a crutch, just as some people subconsciously adopt an illness, a pain, a paralysed arm. Unless you root this out first, you won't succeed with any kind of therapy because you will be working against yourself. Of course if you really do want to change, then you can. You can get in touch with your subconscious to find out whether that part of you wants to change, and if not why not. Enquire what 'rewards' you are getting by not changing. This is how you can do it.

Go to your deep level. Then just put one hand down on your knee and tell yourself that one of your fingers will represent 'yes' and one 'no'. Now ask yourself which will be your 'yes' finger. After a few seconds one of your fingers will almost certainly move. It may give a preliminary tingle and will then probably give a little jump in the air. Follow the same procedure with your 'no' finger. Finally, you can select your 'don't know' finger. Any time you wish to ask your subconscious a question, just ask. This is the way you can learn why you do things, what really motivates your actions. If you want to analyse yourself, this is how you can do it.

Smoking

Let us suppose you honestly decide you want to give up smoking. Go to your deep level and see yourself on your mind screen. You have already recognised that smoking is bad for you. If necessary, you can now convince your subconscious of this and that the rewards of changing are more considerable than anything else. You want to be free of the habit and able to breathe clear, fresh air and be in tune with life.

Picture yourself smoking. You know you are wasting money. Worse, you are damaging your lungs, making your heart work too fast as your whole system strains to reject and destroy the poison you are putting into your body. You see the smoke swirling and the nicotine and tar inside you filling and choking up your lungs. You are aware of the awful smell of stale tobacco on your skin, on your clothes, in your hair. You see those lungs, black and full of tar from years of smoking. With each puff, you can see the tar becoming thicker, spreading to the bronchial tubes and up to the larynx. You hear it rattling as you breathe. And you refuse to have this! You say so. You then destroy that picture.

You see a new picture – of yourself setting a target date on a large calendar. On that ringed day, say a month ahead, you decide you will give up smoking for good. And each time you go to your deep level you renew your pledge to that target date. You tell yourself morning and evening that, from that date, you will never smoke again. And when the target date is reached you will just stop, as you have planned. See yourself looking forward to that target date and your whole brain and body will combine to make it come true. The imagination must be employed to the full. You can be as innovative and creative as you wish in visualising this scenario.

Perhaps a further picture might be useful here, of yourself after the target date being happy and carefree and free from the bondage of smoking.

Alcohol

Deal with alcohol in much the same way as you would with smoking. First ask yourself why you are drinking and realise the benefits of not drinking. You would see the bad aspects and after that the good aspects, the picture of yourself as a sober, responsible person actually enjoying life even more without liquor. Fix a target date on which to stop drinking. Cutting down on drink won't really work; cutting it out is the only satisfactory answer for a person who can finally admit they are dependent on alcohol.

Losing Weight

Being overweight seems a problem for so many people these days because of what we eat and how we eat. Many obese people, of course, have a physical or psychological problem. To put on weight might be a means of 'running away' or of compensating for a lack of love. A little self-analysis would be useful in finding this out. When one finds the cause, that can be dealt with.

However, simply to tackle the harmful weight-producing foods is not difficult. You would destroy these on your mind screen and tell yourself: 'Never again!' Realising and accepting that these foods are harmful, you will simply stop eating them. Instruct yourself that every time you see or think of them you will feel an aversion to them because they would be harmful to your body. See the foods with which you will replace them, knowing they will be good for your body and also good to eat. Decide what would be your ideal weight and size and see yourself reaching such a target and looking the way you want and expect to look. In targeting weight it would be realistic to give yourself a reasonable weekly target, say a reduction of a kilo (two pounds) a week. When you visualise the picture of the self you are striving for, tell yourself how good it will feel to be so slim and able to move and walk lightly and easily.

You would say to yourself:

'I will desire and eat only those foods which are good for my body.'

Meditate on this regularly and you will be successful.

EIGHT

The Health Kick

What Can You Cure?

Did you know that in both England and America there are doctors who claim to cure or alleviate cancer, in some cases, through dynamic meditation? In most of these cases they have probably used other remedies too, such as vitamins and dietary changes, but meditation and visualisation are the main tools.

Many doctors have a very narrow vision, due perhaps to their training and the time factor which does not permit them to look deeply into alternative medicine. And they have to be so busy keeping up with drugs, they haven't the space to learn much about the holistic approach and the real healing energies of the body.

There are, of course, exceptions. One of the best known is Dr Carl Simonton of the USA who discovered that he could work best with patients who had an optimistic attitude to life. Everything in life proceeds from a point of view. Dr Selye, the stress expert, related the story of two boys brought up by an alcoholic father. Years later, a psychologist was investigating the effects of drunkenness on children in broken homes. Separately he asked each son how he had developed as he did. The one was a clean-living teetotaller, the other, like his father, a hopeless drunk. And each gave the identical answer:

'What else would you expect when you've had a father like mine?'

So as you can see, it's not what happens to you in life that makes the difference, but it's the way you react – positively or negatively. And that is what Dr Simonton found to be the case in cancer patients. Dr Ian Pearce in England and also the Bristol Clinic use similar therapies.

The patients most likely to succeed with this meditation-plus-visualisation treatment have a strong basic will to live. In meditation in alpha, they are taught to visualise their tumours and then to visualise their body defences at work and the tumours disappearing. Probably the best way to do this would be to imagine your white cells in action. Whenever there is an injury or invaders have intruded into the body, the white cells swarm there in their thousands. See them going there and mopping up, devouring the mass of soft, grey renegade cells, cleaning them away. If you like, see the white cells with tiny brooms and dustpans or dressed in tiny clean white uniforms, washing the cancer cells away with water and hoses, swabbing out the area and chucking them into soakaway gutters for disposal in the body's waste system – or even swallowing them up. The body does not need exact instructions; it just wants the brain to indicate to it what needs to be done and then see the good, healthy result, the repaired person in action. You don't have to know or visualise correct anatomy – just use imagination to tell the body what needs to be done. It knows how best to go about it. The patient is required to do this three times a day, and there is a very good success rate.

Another visualisation might be to see the cancer cells in the form of discoloured ice-cubes piled up on a plate in front of the patient. If they are then taken and put in the full glare of the sun, the patient can sit and watch them melt away. Patients learn not to see the cancer cells as being strong within an immune system that is too weak. For instance, one would not use the image of a rock gradually being worn down by a stream of healing water – for one thing, the process would take too long. A picture of sandcastles collapsed by the tide would obviously be better. One patient used a gardening visualisation, with her white cells plucking out the weeds – the cancer cells.

Whatever the picture, the session would end with a picture of a complete healing having taken place. This is what the patient is aiming at, the final, full healing and not a partial one.

Strengthening the Immune System

A friend of mine had cancer of the brain, for which she was treated with chemotherapy. The treatment was as usual distressingly unpleasant, though it seemed in this case successful. If she had then known about dynamic meditation she could have lessened the bad side effects by visualising the medicine as defenders aiming weapons against the cancer cells and her body welcoming and accepting the treatment and nullifying its unpleasantness.

Unfortunately, she later developed cancer in the spine and was confined to bed. However, she was an artist with a cheerful nature and worked from her bed so that she could still achieve her artistic goals. At this stage I taught her the whole person, deep level technique. Her brain trouble had left her with an inability to follow numbers so I counted her down merely by using 'deeper' each time a number should have been used, and made a tape for her to use by herself. Very quickly she was up and walking with crutches, and these she was finally able to discard.

She deserved her success and had worked hard. When I had stipulated three times a day, she responded by meditating five times. With such enthusiasm, determination and optimism, it was difficult to fail. She had been getting rid of her wild cancer cells (they are really renegade cells) by letting her good white cells smother them and take them away.

Cancer cells are weak cells and can only get a hold when the patient's normal defences have become weak through something particularly stressful. Then they begin to multiply. But if one can remain calm and determined, there is every chance that the body will start disposing of them. Dr Ian Pearce, a highly qualified medical professional, says we are all likely to get such renegade cells at times, young ones which have forgotten their proper function, perhaps through some chemical imbalance (which can, of course, be stress-related or be due to heavy smoking or even aggravated by dietary abuse of the body). All they retain is their ability to multiply. Usually when this happens, the body's immune system comes into play, just as it would with any 'foreigners' (for example, a virus), and it isolates and destroys them. But when there's a serious dietary deficiency and/or an emotional breakdown through stress of some kind, then the immune system goes to pieces. But the so-called autonomic system, of which the immune system is a part, can be influenced by deep relaxation and meditation.

Thus you can see that what you think is of great importance to your body's health. And what you think deliberately at your deep level will actually get your body moving in the right direction.

Doctors who practise alternative medicine also ask their patients slowly to change to a diet which includes much raw food, especially vegetables and fruit, and to stop eating red meat. In all healing it is important too to rid our minds of any known resentments and hostility. One's mind must be made as peaceful as possible, and meditation and relaxation will, of course, help with that.

More Healing

While cancer is an important matter, there are many other things that badger us – psoriasis, clogged arteries, coughs and colds, headaches, poor eyesight, high or low blood sugar levels, warts and rashes, arthritis, and so on. We cannot guarantee a self-cure for everything, but at some time or another everything has been cured or alleviated by mind, through the power of the brain over the body.

Whatever the condition, you must first learn to relax the body completely, and then visualise it performing well and efficiently. Change on your mind screen whatever is wrong, in whatever creative way you think best. You could perhaps see a bad, ulcerated throat become pink and well. Paint some 'universal white healing balm' on it or spray on a 'healing solution' and gently swab the area with 'universal blue healing solvent'.

Dr Carl Simonton gives the following example in dealing with arthritis:

'First picture your joints very irritated and having little granules on the surfaces. Then see your white blood cells coming in, cleaning up the debris, picking up the little granules and smoothing over the joint surfaces. Then see yourself active, doing what you like to do, free of joint pain.'

Headaches

Here is a fine example of the use of dynamic meditation. I used to get a headache almost every day until I used the alpha plus screen technique. Now, if I get even the faintest glimmer of one, I simply close my eyes and say:

'I don't get headaches any more. Buzz off!'

It took me about a month or so, concentrating on it hard for at least a fortnight and then easing off, just working at it when I felt the odd headache coming again. This was not a migraine but probably a stress-related headache while doing a fairly intensive job. But the relief – and no more pills! It was worth it.

Besides the normal mind screen practice, I also used the time mentally to relax my forehead and neck muscles. Additionally, I used a technique called glove anaesthesia (see page 114).

For migraine, the best technique is to tell yourself that the blood cells in your head will release their blood and send it down to your hands, which will then become warm and heavy. Feel your hands becoming warmer, just as if they were in quite warm water. The blood will come down into your hands and you will almost certainly feel relief in your head.

More White Cell Imagery

One person I know of visualises a tiny golden vacuum cleaner inside her body, buzzing all around the interior, sucking up all dirt, rubbish and unwanted debris from every possible nook and cranny. She leaves it running even when she is not directing it, thus programming continuous cleansing and healing.

Another patient sees her white cells as a flock of pure white goats.

They eat up all rubbish and are strong and tough eaters. Her body she sees as a meadow and the goats are there to keep the place clean. Imagination!

A heart patient saw his troubled blood surging around his heart. The blood was full of sparks of light, reaching everywhere. They were, in fact, his white cells and he visualised them washing over everything, making it all clean and perfect. He would watch until the light sparks quietened down and then saw his blood as calm and healthy again. Imagination!

Imagination

This is your key to your health exercises. Imagine! Imagine whatever seems healing and right, and the process towards improvement and healing will start. We must all remember that the brain is a piece of equipment used by the mind – so use it! Tell the brain what it is you want the body to do. DBE: Desire to heal yourself; Believe it can be done; Expect it to happen – and it will!

Don't forget to make your affirmations too. When you see yourself completely well, tell yourself:

> *'Day by day my disability is getting less and less and I am getting better and better.'*

On your mind screen, watch yourself walking comfortably and flexibly and making all the movements you want. Visualise your body completely free from pain. Tell yourself:

> *'Every day my body will improve in vigour. I feel that life is more purposeful than ever before. I can do and be whatever I want to do or be, provided it does not bring harm to others.'*

Tell yourself that every time you come to your deep level and serene scene you will come there even more quickly, deeply and easily.

This technique is a proper procedure for changing the self from bad to better, from poor to plenty, from sickness to health. In this life you can do what you want to do, achieve what you set out to achieve (but do remember that the journey is far more important than the arrival). In fact, we already do this unconsciously, so why not consciously? If we set out to have riches or a new car, and we concentrate on achieving that, see ourselves doing it, in alpha, then it must happen in due course.

Personally, I consider it is a wasteful use of a wonderful tool to say: 'I want lots of money' or whatever. It is so much better to create the circumstances whereby one can do a good job, produce something worthwhile – something for people to see, read, use, hear or eat – and then the rewards must come. Money is merely the natural token of abundance for doing something well, providing good service, for putting what Solzhenitsyn calls 'duty' before what so many people seem to think of as their 'rights'.

M.E. and the Immune System

It is interesting to note that Dr William Weir, Consultant Physician of the Royal Free Hospital in London, says:

'One of the cornerstones of any therapeutic regimes for M.E. (myalgic encephalomyelitis, also known as chronic fatigue syndrome) involves a regime of rest and relaxation. It is comparatively easy to rest in the strict physical sense, but it is the psychological dimension which eludes many people. A meditation technique is therefore invaluable in this situation as it helps provide the missing dimension. Interestingly, some individuals with M.E. may first experience a transient worsening of their symptoms before noticing an improvement. One explanation for this is that the meditation in some way "switches on" a hitherto unresponsive component of the immune system, enabling it to fight the chronic virus infection present ... With time, these symptoms abate as the immune system clears the offending virus.'

NINE

Your Power House

Moving a Step Further

Once you have fully familiarised yourself with your serene scene and brought it alive, work on it for some time and see the results. When you feel you are ready, you can move from your serene scene to your power house. Don't rush this transition, since the power house concept is a little more advanced. Your brain should easily accept the serene-scene concept because it is based on a scene it has already encountered and is familiar with, which it uses to develop into something out of your imagination. Creating your power house moves you on a stage further.

You are now going to create something that you will be able to use for the rest of your life, although you can always change it if you wish as your own needs change and develop. Your power house is going to be a more concentrated place than your serene scene and, because of this, it will be easier to work there on various projects.

Other people have created such places. Einstein was said to have a mental laboratory where he went to work on different problems. The writer Napoleon Hill had a 'cabinet room' and used mentally to consult several famous people there. I myself used to have a private room in my mind for passive meditation, then I created another for dynamic meditation. At first I actually used to lock the door to my passive meditation room; that's how real it was for me. Eventually, I realised this was rather ridiculous and dismantled the lock! The room I created for passive meditation was structured from clear, unbreakable glass and built on top of a mountain. Eventually, I decided that I no longer needed one room for passive and one room for dynamic meditation, so I decided to combine them. However, that was right for me at the time, and it may be the same for you.

It really doesn't matter where you construct your power house or what it is built of – brick, stone, wood, glass, whatever. You can construct and furnish it in any way you like. I had one pupil who built her power house under the sea because that is what she found most effective. To reach her special room, she first had to take herself to a small island, then go down below the ocean to reach her power house.

Creating Your Power House

This is how you can create your personal power house. Go to your deep level and then go even deeper inside yourself, counting yourself down to the deepest level. As we have seen this will deepen with practice and may be deep alpha or even theta. Then begin to tell yourself that from this deep level of consciousness, you have the power to do anything your imagination can conceive, as long as it is always for the good of yourself and others.

Now visualise yourself walking down three steps and then create in your mind's eye a door in front of you. It can be any sort of door you like, wherever you want it to be and in whatever surroundings you choose as this is the entrance to your unique power house. Think about the most appropriate image for you personally; what you want is what matters in this visualisation. Once you have created your power house, this is the route you will take to reach it: go down to the deep level in your mind and walk down those three steps to your power house door.

Now open the door and go inside. Visualise yourself as really there; feel you are actually in your special place and creating the four main walls and the ceiling and floor of your personal power house. Take a little time to create this room exactly as you want it. You can make it whatever size and shape you want, but leave one wall clear because this is where your mind screen will be. Use whatever materials you like, and have a window or windows as you wish. The lighting will come on automatically as you enter the room, though you can always control it. For example, if you are using the room for passive meditation, you may want to dim the light; that is all in the control of your mind. The temperature of the room will always be comfortable. Remember that you are both architect and builder so the details are yours to command. And, of course, if you want to add, change or remodel, you can do so at any time you are in your power house level.

When you are in alpha deep level, time has a different quality and probably five minutes will be ample to erect your power house. When it is done you will be ready to furnish it.

The one thing you will definitely need is, of course, your mind screen. This will be quite large and will light up well whenever you use it. You will be able to see anything or anyone (including yourself) on the screen in three dimensions, in full length or close up, and still or moving, as you wish. You can screen a personal movie on it to review some incident in the past or to project yourself into the future to plan total success, as well as seeing the present, of course.

Put a carpet on the floor if you want, or choose polished wood and rugs. Hang curtains or blinds at the windows or choose to have an uninterrupted view of the scene outside. Place pictures on the walls if that makes the room more comfortable and personal. You will need at least one comfortable chair and perhaps a nice desk or table. You will usually sit in your chair when you are in your power house, so make it just the kind you want so you can sit comfortably in it while watching your screen. It is a good idea to have a panel built into the arm of the chair for your screen controls – one to produce new pictures and the second one to destroy them.

If you are imaginative enough, you can, of course, have a radio on your desk so that you can listen to your favourite music while you are in your power house. There are many other devices you may wish to have accessible; perhaps even a delicate brush to sweep away any germs, infection, or even facial lines you don't want. Have a whole array behind you of special lotions for applying to any injury for cleansing and fast healing, and label them with names to activate your imagination: 'Universal Throat Paint', 'Universal Arthritis Paint' or 'Universal Anaesthetic Ointment', perhaps. In fact, you can use anything you can imagine or invent.

To the right of your screen, in the far wall, I suggest you construct a door. You may at some time invite someone in to assist you – a doctor, a counsellor? – or you may go through there yourself, as I'll explain later.

Your First Exercise

If you go and sit down in your power house and observe your screen light up, you will be able to visualise yourself on it. See the image as though it is a moving X-ray of yourself. As you watch, see your skull, the eyes in your skull, and your jawbone, and then see inside your neck and the bones in your shoulders. Glance down and see your digestive tract going down to your stomach, and then see your respiratory tract going down to your lungs, which are breathing rhythmically. See your ribs and, behind them, glimpse your heart beating in a normal and natural rhythm. Then move your eyes slowly down your body, becoming aware of each organ, then down your arms and fingers, your thighs, calves, ankles and toes.

The next stage is to turn your body around on your screen and repeat the process of looking slowly over every inch in the reverse order, working from the toes right up to the top of the skull.

What you are checking for is anything which is out of the ordinary, any signs that you have some physical health problem. At deep level in your power house, you will be able to see and identify any problems as you encounter them in your search through your body. You can use this method to examine yourself at any time if you think you may have a health problem of any sort so that you can discover what is wrong and start healing it. Remember that if you do suspect any health problems, you should also consult your doctor.

Power House Meditation Technique

This summary of the technique is designed to help you practise your own power house meditation technique and supports the full information in the text. As you develop your technique, you will gradually personalise your own approach.

- Sit comfortably and relax your body (see page 64).
- Breathe in and out deeply two or three times.
- Move down to the alpha level.
- Count yourself down further to an even deeper level of consciousness.
- Tell yourself you have the power to do anything your imagination can conceive.
- Walk down three steps to the door of your power house.
- Open the door and go inside your power house.
- To begin, work on your room until it is created and furnished exactly as you want it, with a mind screen, a comfortable chair and a door in the far wall.
- Sit comfortably in your power house and feel relaxed and at peace.
- Light up your mind screen.
- Press the first button on your control panel.
- Project your first, negative picture on to the mind screen and experience the scene.
- Press the second button on your control panel.
- See the image disintegrate.
- Project the positive image on to the mind screen and experience the scene.
- Complete your meditation.
- Count yourself up to beta levels.

How do you go about the healing process? Again, using the power of your mind and an image which is appropriate to you. First, try just seeing and feeling a powerful healing energy entering your head and moving down right through your body. You could experience it as a white or a golden light pouring into you, or a shower washing over and into your body and spreading its cleansing and healing power. Whatever image works for you is the one which you should use; there are no rights and wrongs.

Once you have gone through this process, take your time to relax and then count yourself up to your conscious level. Do this regularly until you can no longer see the problem – you will have washed it away with the cleansing power of your mind and your imagination.

Once you have successfully tried out this exercise – even if it is only on a mild headache – you will know that if you use your power house and your tools properly you can programme yourself for health at any time you need.

What Else Can I Achieve?

Having seen this exercise work and practised it in your power house, you will be able to do the same thing for other problems in your life. The principle of using your mind screen is the same one as when you are in your serene scene but, as I have said, the effect of working at one more remove and at a deeper level makes the process more potent.

Do you wish to change an aspect of your character which is creating problems in your life? Once you have identified the problem, work through the process of going down to your deep alpha level and visiting your power house. Switch on your mind screen and set to work. Visualise an existing situation: something which has happened or which you can see will happen in a set of circumstances if things remain as they are. See yourself as tongue-tied at a job interview or not being able to express your real self to someone you would like to get to know better. Live that situation on your mind screen. Then destroy it at the touch of the destruct button.

Then bring your mind screen to life again, this time with an image of how the situation will be when you have made the changes you desire. Live every minute of that new scenario until you are so familiar with it that you believe that is how it will be. Remember: Desire, Believe, Expect. It can and will happen because you can make it happen.

TEN

The Hub of Life

In *Religion and the Rebel*, Colin Wilson said:

> *'How can man extend his range of consciousness? I believe that human beings experience a range of mental states which is as narrow as the middle three notes of a piano keyboard. I believe that the possible range of mental states is as wide as the whole piano keyboard, and that man's sole aim and business is to extend his range from the usual three or four notes to the whole keyboard.'*

So how do we go about activating the rest of our mental keyboard so that we can really begin to reach our potential? I believe that passive meditation is the key, and to underline how important passive meditation is to finding our place in the universe and activating our full potential, I would like to give you some examples of how various deep-thinking and influential people view the subject.

Herbert Puryear, in *Reflections on the Path* (which deals with the readings of American seer and healer Edgar Cayce), said that meditation — by which he meant passive meditation — is not only the hub of healing but should be the hub of our lives. Yet, he added, it may be the most talked-about and least practised of the activities recommended by every spiritual teacher.

When asked by Fritjof Capra:

'How can I be a scientist and still follow your advice of stopping thought and attaining freedom from the known?'

Krishnamurti replied:

'First you are a human being; then you are a scientist. First you have to become free and this freedom cannot be achieved through thought. It is achieved through meditation – the understanding of the totality of life in which every form of fragmentation has ceased.'

Scientists specialise in one specific part of life, but they first need to see and understand life as a whole so that they can then realise just where their speciality fits into the overall scheme. When you meditate, you are in the centre of consciousness and therefore you can begin to understand life as a whole.

'Meditation,' wrote Aldous Huxley, *'has been used in every part of the world, and from the remotest periods, as a method for acquiring knowledge about the essential nature of things.'*

A young graduate student on his way to a meditation course said:

'It's the greatest adventure of all. You don't know what you're going to find, but whatever it is you know it's going to change your life.'

This is the open-minded concept with which I believe you should approach passive meditation.

'Meditation is not an escape from daily living,' said the writer Ardis Whitman, *'but a preparation for it, and what is of surpassing importance is what we bring back from the experience.'*

He also wrote:

'Meditation is not a cure-all. Properly used, however, it can give us back the wonderland of our minds ... Today there is a widespread feeling that the world of tomorrow should be very different from the world of today. Meditation is seen as a prelude to that

transformation – a way of preparing for it, a way of changing lives and thus changing the world.'

The psychologist Erich Fromm, when asked for a practical solution to the problems of living, replied:

'Quietness. The experience of stillness. You have to stop in order to be able to change direction.'

Is Meditation Religion?

A dictionary definition of religion is:

'A belief in a superhuman being or beings, especially a personal god, controlling the universe and entitled to worship and obedience, and the feelings, effects on conduct and the practices resulting from such belief.'

Meditation is therefore not religion in itself, as religion involves the whole structure and doctrine of the belief in a supernatural force.

However, if the concept interests you, then it is productive to think about it and to think about what meditation is. Is it simply a way to learn to allay tension (which, of course, it can)? Is it only a method of improving your health? If you believe that it is, you need only concern yourself with the practice of dynamic (or practical) meditation, which we have been considering. If, on the other hand, you are not afraid to face or accept the possibility – even the probability, some would say – of there being a directing force outside yourself, a universal consciousness of which you are a part, then you can do no harm, but only good, by opening yourself to that consciousness. It is my belief that passive meditation is the way of opening that door to a universal directing force.

Using Passive Meditation

As an introduction to this concept, Herbert Puryear gives an illustration of how he uses meditation:

> *'As I meditate in the morning, my mind drifts off to an afternoon job interview about which I am concerned. First, I acknowledge the fact of my mind drifting.'*

In fact, he does not stop the drift because he is unwittingly seeking a solution to a problem and seizes the opportunity to do so which is offered to him. But it is possible to stop the 'drift' of stray thoughts if you wish, as I shall show you later.

> *'Second,'* he goes on, *'I invite the spirit of Christ – or God – to stand between me and the situation. I say: "Lord, this is important. I know it can be handled only in Your presence. I cannot handle it but I know You can." And third, I say: "Because this is important, it is all the more reason why I need to take these few moments to become centred ... " In an ongoing practice of meditation, we begin to put our concerns into relationship with the divine and release the concern to him. For example, let's say that every Thursday afternoon you have an appointment with Joe, with whom you are having difficulties. In your meditation during the week, if your mind drifts off to your concern with Joe, you try to sense the presence of the [universal power] in this relationship. In your next meeting with him, instead of making the usual negative responses, you will find yourself responding to him with a more loving attitude. Why? Because you have relinquished your anxiety. You know that there is another power working in the relationship. You are more loving and Joe responds by being more co-operative.'*

In this context, the Santa Fe Stress Clinic recommends that after meditation you use a technique which they call 'Fill your heart with loving thoughts'.

> *'A loving heart,'* they say, *'will help to heal many of our ills. Begin with thoughts of family and friends. They are easier to love, usually, than strangers or enemies. As a face appears before you, or a name, send your blessings and loving thoughts to that person. Then devote some time to sending loving thoughts to those who may be causing you some disturbance. Try to understand clearly that they are fumbling through life as we all are and our anger and bitterness towards them only hurts us all. Forgive and forget so that you can be free of anger. The two or three minutes you put into sending out*

loving thoughts is very important and you will reap tremendous benefit to your state of health as well as your peace of mind.'

Edgar Cayce, asked by a patient if he could receive guidance from meditation, replied:

'On any subject! Whether you are going digging for worms or playing a concerto.'

Dr Puryear comments:

'The answer to every question, every problem, is within; there is no question too great or too small to bring to the one within.'

He adds:

'Some worry about the dangers of meditation, but let us say that the only thing more dangerous than meditating is not meditating.'

Ramala, whose messages have been received through channelling, in *The Revelations of Ramala*, says much the same:

'As you are faced with the problems of the day, you should consciously tune into the higher self ... Meditation is the key to your evolution. It is the only key for, until you have unlocked the door to your higher consciousness, truly you will not discover the meaning of life on this earth.'

Finally, before explaining the technique of passive meditation, consider Dr Puryear's interesting summing-up of the reason why the power to meditate was given to us:

'In the study of biology one finds that the human body is fantastically adapted to life on the earth. It is a special instrument for coping with and expressing mastery and creativity in the earth plane. It is also another special kind of instrument. We may think of it as God's special solution to a problem: His children as spiritual beings cutting themselves off from the awareness of His nature. Because we had been placed in a three-dimensional plane, it became necessary to develop an instrument that could manifest in such a plane, and yet one which had the capability for the awareness of oneness with the infinite. There had to be the sensory potentiality for experiencing that awareness in consciousness.'

This capability of awareness with the whole, a way of becoming aware of our oneness with our creator, of silent communication, of receiving 'input', is the true purpose of passive meditation.

Spiritual Progress

If you are concerned with spiritual progress, you will be interested in what Joel Goldsmith, an inspired healer and teacher, had to say:

'Without meditation it is difficult, if not almost impossible, to make spiritual progress, because spiritual attainment is accomplished in the mind. It was revealed to me that the best way to attain divine consciousness lies in meditation ... To attain through meditation, there must first of all be an agreement within one's self that in the meditation there is no seeking for any thing or condition, but a seeking only for the illumined mind ...'

Although this seems a slightly different viewpoint to others we have mentioned, it must be remembered that Joel Goldsmith was concerned very strictly with pure spiritual progress for the individual and nothing else. Ideally, if you have learnt simply to 'hand over' in deepest faith, he is probably correct.

On the question of illumination, Dr Raynor Johnson, in *A Religious Outlook for Modern Man*, says:

'Mystical experience, in which for a moment the centre of the soul contacts a reality higher than oneself – the spirit – is a state of illumination which we are all seeking, whether we know it or not. Everything that we can desire in our highest moments is satisfied in this union ... The goal of mind control is important; the particular method used to reach the goal is not ... Those who have trodden this path and finally come to glimpse the Reality which lies beyond mind tell us that it is unforgettable, peaceful, satisfying, and blissful beyond the power of words to describe ... But whatever inner discipline is undertaken, the outer life has concurrently to be lived in the right way ... If a person's daily round is dull and uninspiring, let him say: "I do it gladly because it is my duty; I do it because it is my offering of service to God."

'If a person's daily round is interesting, let them in gratitude offer their work as a service to God, not concerned with benefit to themselves but with help to others.'

Meditation Plus Thought Control

Now we have looked at the purposes of passive meditation, let's see how it can actually be done. If you find it helpful, you can make a recording of your meditation techniques and use that for a while as you familiarise yourself with the procedures, otherwise you can just use your own words and thoughts.

Go to your deep alpha level and step down your three steps to your power house. Open the door and sit in your chair, facing your mind screen. This time, however, you are not in your power house to work on a change in yourself but to contact the stillness that is at your centre.

As you sit in your chair, slowly dim the lights a little to a comfortable, subtle level. Close your eyes and feel at peace, knowing that you are going to sit there in the quiet of your inner room, your refuge, and you are going simply to be aware. Don't force anything to happen, just feel deeply at peace with the mind as still as possible. If anything comes to you, it will simply happen and you will experience it and enjoy it; otherwise you will sit in peace and stillness and with absolute calm in your mind. This is passive meditation – getting in touch with your inner self.

While you are meditating, casual thoughts may arise from your brain. If they do, watch the thought float up by your head and immediately put a 'balloon' around it – mentally draw a line around the thought and so encase it. As soon as you do, the thought will drift away from you, float away and vanish. Do this whenever a thought occurs to distract you from your inner peace. If it is a troublesome thought or vision, you can just pop the balloon with your finger.

An alternative is to imagine your mind as a piece of glass on which your thought picture arrives. You can then wipe it away with a mental windscreen wiper. Another technique is to breathe fast four times, in and out, and the thought will disappear.

A final method is to put invisible armour around your head, or surround your head with a white light, through which no thought can penetrate. Use whichever method most appeals to you.

Soon you will find that thoughts become discouraged and will stop coming. In this way you can control the production of thought, and then you will be able to sit in contact with your inner self and experience that feeling of peace, joy or any other good experience which comes to you.

Often when you come to your power house like this, you will feel and know that there is a presence there with you, a higher self, a seen or unseen presence or teacher whom you can consult when you feel the need. That presence is there only when you ask and has only your good in mind.

You know that you can have this experience of meditation whenever you wish. You can sit there as long as you wish, or you can set a time limit if you instruct yourself that you want to limit the time spent in meditation. Or you can just decide when it is time to move from your power house because your mind, though still and at peace, is ready to return to the beta level. When that happens, you can easily go back to your outer level by slowly counting up from one to five in the usual way, knowing you will feel totally refreshed and invigorated when you open your eyes on the count of five.

Beyond Meditation

After you have experienced true passive meditation, I would like you to try one final step, something a little more advanced still. Go to your deep level as before and then down the steps into your power house. From there, I will show you how to go beyond meditation, to go outwards instead of inwards.

In your power house, stand up and go forward and walk to the door on the right of your screen. Open the door, and as you do so create a balcony on to which you can go. Walk on to the balcony and experience the fact that you are high up, high above the Earth, which you can see below you when you look down. You could be in the clouds or above the clouds, or high above mountains – as always, it is your choice.

Passive Meditation Technique

This summary of the technique is designed to help you practise your own passive meditation technique and supports the full information in the text. As you develop your technique, you will gradually personalise your own approach.

- *Sit comfortably and relax your body (see page 64).*
- *Breathe in and out deeply two or three times.*
- *Move down to the alpha level.*
- *Count yourself down further to an even deeper level of consciousness.*
- *Tell yourself you have the power to do anything your imagination can conceive.*
- *Walk down three steps to the door of your power house.*
- *Open the door and go inside your power house.*
- *Sit comfortably in your power house and feel relaxed and at peace.*
- *Dim the lights, feel at peace and be aware.*
- *Capture any distracting thoughts and banish them from your mind.*
- *Experience the inner joy of being in contact with your inner self.*
- *Open your mind to a higher presence.*
- *Complete your meditation.*
- *Count yourself up to beta levels.*

Sit down on a chair on your balcony and tell yourself you are going to a deeper level than ever before. You are going deeper and deeper within yourself. You can feel that you are at a much deeper level of consciousness than you were before, and it is a very good, strong feeling.

Now you are going to leave your body sitting on the balcony for a while as your mind goes out to join the power of the life force which is there. Say to yourself, 'There is only God; there is only God's power,' which is an absolute protection for you. Then feel that your mind moves and goes out from your body to that great power so that you become one with it, listening and aware, and open to experience anything which comes to you and which can only be good.

As you do this, you will be conscious that your mind is now high above the Earth. You will be aware that all things on the earthly sphere pass with time and that while you are part of that earthly sphere, you are also part of the eternal whole. You will feel cherished and unique, part of the great unity of all things and beings on the Earth and within the universe, yet also part of the infinite, which is immortal. Because you have gone beyond the Earth, nothing that happens on the Earth is any of your concern while you are part of the universal mind.

As you remain there, you will experience the knowledge that you can come there and experience this feeling whenever you wish and for as long as you wish. As before, you can go back to your outer level whenever you are ready by counting yourself up from one to five. When you return to your normal level of waking consciousness, you will feel very well, refreshed, alert and full of energy.

Beyond Meditation Technique

This summary of the technique is designed to help you practise your own technique and supports the full information in the text. As you develop your technique, you will gradually personalise your own approach.

- *Sit comfortably and relax your body (see page 64).*
- *Breathe in and out deeply two or three times.*
- *Move down to the alpha level.*
- *Count yourself down further to an even deeper level of consciousness.*
- *Tell yourself you have the power to do anything your imagination can conceive.*
- *Walk down three steps to the door of your power house.*
- *Open the door and go inside your power house.*
- *Sit comfortably in your power house and feel relaxed and at peace.*
- *Go through the door to a balcony high above the Earth and sit down.*
- *Take yourself deeper within yourself.*
- *Leave your body as your mind goes out to join the power of the life force.*
- *Experience the unity of all things on Earth and the feeling of being part of the infinite.*
- *Complete your meditation.*
- *Count yourself up to beta levels.*

ELEVEN

Additional Techniques

Self-hypnosis

On page 45 in Chapter 4, I referred briefly to going into a lower brain rhythm for self-instruction. Normally you would not need this depth, but it can be useful in certain circumstances. If you experience an emergency situation – a sudden pain or injury that you want to deal with quickly and in deep concentration – you could use the technique I will describe. Sometimes I use it to induce sleep in the middle of the night if I wake up and thoughts start whirling around in my mind and prevent me from sleeping.

Tell yourself that you are going to induce self-hypnosis and that it will, in the case of wishing to sleep, automatically take you into a normal, deep sleep until your usual waking time in the morning. The following is the best and simplest method I have discovered.

First, tell yourself you are going to count up to ten and that you will then be in a state of hypnotic sleep. Open your eyes and strain them a little by looking upwards without moving your head. As soon as your eyes begin to tire, close them and say 'one' to yourself. Open them again, repeat the process but say 'two'. Continue tiring your eyes by looking upwards, then relaxing and closing them and saying 'three', then 'four', and so on. You will find that the length of time you leave your eyes open will become progressively shorter until you feel as though you would rather not open them again – probably at about the count of five. Carry on counting without opening your eyes again and at ten, tell yourself you are now in a state of self-hypnosis. Finish by telling yourself that you will fall into a deep and refreshing sleep and awaken at your normal time feeling rested and energised.

If you are using self-hypnosis for any reason other than to sleep, you can instruct your body as you wish. For example, you could say, 'The pain in my leg is going away now and my natural body defences will work quickly to repair any damage.' Concentrate on that feeling for a short while – perhaps a few minutes – and then, when you feel more comfortable, tell yourself that your leg will continue to improve as you open your eyes. Then, of course, you could add whatever treatment you would normally give.

Glove Anaesthesia

An alternative way of dealing with pain is to induce what is called 'glove anaesthesia'. You can use this process to anaesthetise one hand but it is simplest to do it with one finger – probably your first or index finger.

Go into self-hypnosis as before and tell yourself that your finger is going to become desensitised and numb, without any feeling. As you repeat this statement to yourself, try to sense the finger losing all feeling. It will probably begin to tingle, then it will gradually lose all feeling. Practise this a few times until you become proficient. Test it by pressing your thumbnail into your finger. When it feels fairly numb, instruct yourself that when you touch whatever part of your body is painful, the anaesthesia will transfer itself to that part. Talk to yourself as you rub your finger over the affected area, stressing that you are anaesthetising wherever you rub and that the anaesthetic will affect not just the surface level but also the area below the skin. Instruct yourself that the effect will last until healing begins.

Glove anaesthesia works very well for headaches. Tell yourself you are transferring the sensation of anaesthesia from the first finger to the site of your headache and touch your head at the source of the pain. Practise the technique and you will find that it becomes increasingly effective.

Four-step Problem Solving

This is a non-meditative technique which I recalled when I was treating someone for back trouble. It is a handing-over technique which I first published in a tiny booklet. However, I then realised that it would be even more effective if done in alpha.

I had gone to see June, a woman of about 50, who had a history of appalling back trouble. She had undergone two operations and many scans, X-rays and other diagnostic tests and treatments. When I met her, she was in almost constant pain. You could see the pain in her eyes and from the wastage of her body. The doctors could not find a physical cause for the pain she was experiencing and had given her up as a case of psychosomatic illness.

I tried to induce her into meditation, even hypnosis, but though she tried, she was simply not able to concentrate. Whenever I went to see her – she was limited to movement around her flat – she spent what little time we had together railing against fate, the many doctors she had seen, and her husband, whose tolerance and help had worn thin – he was just not strong enough to be the rock she needed. In short she was – or had become – a very negative person. I was even afraid she might try to take her own life, although fortunately this did not happen. I began to feel that there was little I could do.

I fully sympathised with her and understood the circumstances which had made her so negative, but slowly I became less sympathetic and less understanding – rather like her husband, I suppose. Eventually, I had to tell her there was little I could do. If she wasn't so negative, I thought, she might be able to start on a positive recovery programme. She might never be fully cured even then, but her problem could become more tolerable. That was my thinking at the time. The story would be pointless if that opinion did not change!

I have a weakness in my lower back and one day I lifted a particularly heavy garden pot full of earth. I moved it blithely from left to right and my body was wrongly placed for the movement. I was an idiot. I felt something give. Two days later, I was in agony and could hardly move for fear of going into spasm.

In bed I tried to meditate and succeeded to some degree – after all, I have had a lot of experience. But the pain in my back became worse. Things sometimes do at first, stirred by new energies, but I hadn't come near to being able to give myself a proper treatment. Two days later, still in bed, I became morose and depressed. I did not know what I had done to my back. I had thought I'd pulled a muscle, perhaps torn some tissue. Now I began to think I had done something much worse, perhaps slipped a disc, crushed a nerve. My whole middle was on fire. It was painful to get up, painful to lie down, and when I moved about at all I merely crept. Perhaps I would never recover properly. I lay still and could scarcely think.

Suddenly I remembered June – was this what she felt like? How could I have expected her, without previous introduction or training, to be positive! And now here was I – with all my knowledge and experience of meditation and healing – giving up.

Then I remembered my little four-step problem-solving technique. A way to hand over. I needed it.

Step 1: You have a seemingly insoluble problem. Clearly visualise in your mind the problem or condition which needs healing or changing.

Step 2: Imagine a key with, at the top, a circle containing a cross or any other symbol of infinite power. Tell yourself:

'There is a key to every problem.'

Step 3: Move your eyes and mind up to that symbol and say:

'I now release this problem to infinite power in the certainty that it will be resolved. I know I can hand over this problem in this way and, because I so ask, it is already being resolved.'

Step 4: To demonstrate your faith, give thanks for the solution or healing which is to come.

At once I carried out the four-step process and immediately I felt better. The pain was still there but my mind cleared. I felt positive and I knew that it was only a matter of patience and my back would get better. Then I could perform my mind screen healing with ease and with absolute knowledge of positive results to come, as they did.

Helping Others

You can use the four-step technique for helping others. In meditation you can also often help or even heal others.

In a meditative state, you can send healing energy out to others who are in need. Visualise the energy beam however it suits you. I myself like a golden beam of healing energy, although some prefer to use a white light. You can also surround your house or car or others with the healing beam of protection.

You can also send 'thought forms', as long as they are for the benefit of others and not merely yourself. For instance, if you know someone with a very difficult child, or perhaps someone who has to cope with a troublesome adult, you can visualise that person and transmit suggestions for better behaviour. Visualise events as if they are actually happening. The more explicit you are, the more likely they are to be effective.

In this way, there is no end to the good you can achieve both for yourself and for others.

Don't delay – meditate today.

Index

Jefferies, Richard 8–9
Jesus Christ 18, 21
Johnson, Raynor *A Religious Outlook for Modern Man* 106–7

Kampf, Harold 7–8, 10, 11–12
Kant, Immanuel 9
Krishna 10
Krishnamurti, Jiddu 102

latihan 7–8
LeShan, Lawrence 36
life
  aims in 17–19
  changing 13, 49–59, 76–84
life force 31–2, 37, 110
  see also God; higher power; higher self; power of good
lifestyle, changing 81–4
love 19

Mandus, Brother *This Wondrous Way of Life* 30–31
masks 15–16, 21
Maslow, Abraham 8
M.E. (myalgic encephalomyelitis) 91
medicine, holistic 85–91
meditation 7, 14, 75–6
  ABC ultimate technique 63, 69–71, 74
  beyond meditation 108, 110–11
  counting down to 67, 70
  counting up from 72–3
  dynamic 15, 29, 57, 76–80, 85–91
  effects of 10
  and God 35–41, 103–7, 110
  and health 85–91, 96, 98
  methods 45
  need for 30
  passive 15, 18, 29, 101–11
  and prayer 30–32
  and religion 32–3, 103–7
  techniques 63
  types of 29–30
  speed 15
  Subud 7–8

whole person deep level technique 63, 66–8
  see also alpha state; self–hypnosis; visualisation
migraines 89
  see also headaches
mind 27, 43–4
mind screen 77–8, 80
  power house 95, 96, 98–9
Mother Teresa of Calcutta 19
mysticism, Christian 11

needs 17, 58
negative emotions 16–17, 56
negative thoughts 115
Nietzsche, Friedrich 11

passive meditation 15, 18, 29, 101–3
  technique 107–8, 109
  using 103–6
peace 19
peak experiences 8–9
Pearce, Dr Ian 86, 87–8
permanent high 58–9
physical relaxation 43–4, 61–3, 64
pleasure 17–18
  short-term 20
positive thinking 76–7, 90–91
  power of 44
  see also self-hypnosis; visualisation
power
  given to others 20, 25
  higher 29, 30
  over self 15
power house 93–4
  beyond meditation 108, 110–11
  creating 94–6
  doors 108, 110–11
  furnishing 94–5
  and health 96, 98
  meditation technique 96–9
  visualisation of 94–6
power of good 36–8
  handing over to 38–41
  separation from 38

Also Available from Quantum

(An Imprint of W. Foulsham & Co. Ltd.)

Swimming with Dolphins
A Healing Experience

by Lisa Tenzin Dolma

'His eye looked straight into my eyes, and I gazed back. This was the most beautiful feeling I have ever experienced. I cried ... from a feeling of euphoric freedom.'

This magical book is an uplifting account of close encounters with dolphins. Fifteen amazing personal accounts reveal the mysterious qualities of these very special creatures: ESP, intelligence, sensitivity, astonishing benevolence, communication and their role as healers.

Swimming with dolphins is a joyous experience.

ISBN 0-572-02364-2

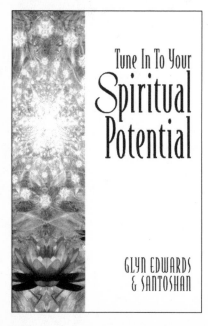

Tune in to your Spiritual Potential

by Glyn Edwards and Santoshan

'Seek your *spirit* on its terms ... and develop your hidden potential.'

You can develop your dormant spiritual abilities to the level of your choice. With these tried-and-tested techniques and daily exercise regime, you can achieve an immeasurably positive change in your life.

Start today, no matter how busy you are or how much pressure you are under, and become more peaceful, positive and successful, living *in* your world, not inhibited *by* it. It is what you do from now on that's important.

With this book, the present and future hold many exciting possibilities. You have only to take this opportunity to change your life wondrously.

ISBN 0-572-02510-6

Anyone Can Dowse for Better Health

by Arthur Bailey

Arthur Bailey, a qualified engineer, approached dowsing somewhat sceptically. As a scientist, he found the theory incredible. But today, after many hundreds of blind and double-blind trials, Arthur Bailey has written this book to introduce the power of dowsing to others.

Dowsing can enable you to identify your personal coding system which gives you the means to test yourself for food sensitivities and also reveal the minerals and supplements in which you are lacking. When necessary, you can even dowse your own alternative medicines.

ISBN 0-572-02461-4

The Colour Guide to Crystal Healing

by J S Stuart

'If you are looking for a primer in crystal therapy, this is the book for you.'

Every crystal produces its own unique energy, some of which will be more beneficial to you and your psyche than others. Your intuition and zodiac influences will play their part in your selection, and often a selection of these energies are what you need to produce a therapeutic effect.

This book sets out to identify the combinations of crystal energies that are right for each individual's need. From Agate to Zircon we look, in colour, at the most popular healing crystals and their application in massage, meditation and holistic well-being.

ISBN 0-572-02257-3

Quantum and Foulsham titles are available from all good booksellers.